EYE SHOT

40 YEAR SEARCH FOR THE TRUTH

TOM CURRY

CONTENTS

DEDICATION	7
ACKNOWLEDGEMENTS	8
FOREWORD	9
AUTHOR'S INTRODUCTION	12
CHAPTER 1 NEWS ARTICLE 29 JAN 1991	15
CHAPTER 2 GARY'S BRIEF ACCOUNT OF BEING SHOT	19
Author's Comment	22
CHAPTER 3 INJURED ON-DUTY OFFICERS	23
PC David Rathband (Late)	25
Darren Rathband's Quote	27
Author's Comment	29
John Hadfield (Late)	29
Author's Comment	32
Pam White	32
Author's Comment	34
Harrods' Bomb	35
Simon Bywater	37
Author's Comment	40
Sue Mitchell	41
Author's Comment	45
Andrew Hutchison	45
Author's Comment	48
Tracy Mather	49
Author's Comment	50
Andy Walker	51

Anonymous GMP Female Serving Officer..54
Author's Comment 54
John O'Rourke..55
Author's Comment 58
CHAPTER 4 GARY'S EARLY YEARS 60
George Pearson (Late) 63
Florence Pearson (Late) 66
Dean Pearson (Late)..74
CHAPTER 5 GARY'S POLICE STORIES..76
Woolworth's Fire 114
Pope John Paul II...120
CHAPTER 6 GARY IS RUSHED TO HOSPITAL..129
The Guinea Pig Club 132
Pete Ramsden...143
Author's Comment 144
CHAPTER 7 GARY RETURNS TO DUTY..146
CHAPTER 8 LIFE AFTER THE POLICE 152
CHAPTER 9 GARY FULLY RETIRES...158
CHAPTER 10 COLD CASE REVIEW...166
Gary Pearson's Witness Statement 166
Firearms Expert's Report: Dated 11 April 1985 Commissioned By Gary Pearson
....171
Kevin Moore's Conclusions...179
Tom Curry's Conclusions...184
Update 186
Important Revelation. 13 October 2024...191
CHAPTER 11 BREAKING NEWS...195
Author's Comment 200
CHAPTER 12 BOOK CONCLUSION 201
THE FINAL WORDS ARE LEFT TO GARY..207
Books by the same author:...210

DEDICATION

Dedicated to Gary Pearson, his wife and family.

ACKNOWLEDGEMENTS

Gary Pearson, Kevin Moore, Darren Rathband,

And all who have contributed to this book.

FOREWORD

I have known Tom Curry for many years, indeed ever since the mid-1980s when he was a serving police constable at Hastings, Sussex and I was a detective constable working from the same station. Tom was an 'old school bobby' with an acute 'copper's nose' for the suspicious and with a determination to do right by any victim. Whilst he may have ceased to be a police officer, his sense of justice is as keen as ever and he remains active in this area.

I formed a liking for Tom in those days due to his proactive work as a uniformed patrol officer leading to him making many arrests a number of which he then passed on to me to further those investigations. I admired his tenacity and determination to do right by the public we served. Roll forward a good many years and Tom became a member of the local Eastbourne & District Branch of NARPO (National Association of Retired Police Officers) of which I am the secretary.

Tom has previously successfully written an autobiography which he self-published and after this not insignificant project, he moved on to other things.

I became aware of his campaign to secure the award of a medal for those police officers who had unfortunately been injured on duty and who had then been medically retired prior to them being able to achieve the length of service required for them to receive the 'Long Service and Good Conduct Medal'.

Quite rightly, Tom identified the fact that officers themselves had often been let down by the police organisation which had on many occasions failed to recognise their service and had often overlooked their acts of bravery leading to them sustaining their injuries.

He has been instrumental in attracting the support of key members of parliament and other opinion formers in an attempt to achieve formal recognition of the service performed by those officers sadly medically retired.

He also wrote his second book again self-published and very successful entitled 'Dysfunctional Police Family Add Insult to Injury'. I was pleased to be able to write the foreword to that book.

Tom, with the assistance of others, set up a Facebook group called 'Campaign for Medal Recognition for Injured U.K. Police Officers' in an effort to publicise the campaign further.

It was as a result of the Facebook group that former and serving injured police officers began to share their stories. Some actively sought out Tom knowing he had an interest and was more than willing to hear their experiences.

Since creating that Facebook group, he has extended this coverage through Facebook to include the fire and ambulance services thus involving all emergency service personnel who have had the misfortune to be medically retired from the occupations they loved due to injuries sustained whilst working.

Many of the accounts are harrowing but none more so than that of

Greater Manchester police officer, Gary Pearson, who was shot in the face, lost an eye and required major facial reconstruction and who is the subject of this book.

I was pleased to achieve the rank of detective chief superintendent, and I was the senior investigating officer (SIO) in many major criminal cases throughout my career, including those involving murder.

Tom approached me to write the foreword for this book. In addition, he requested that I examine the available evidence of Gary Pearson's shooting as I have done many times in my career with numerous so-called 'Cold Cases'. This I have done, and my conclusions are detailed within this book.

Finally, whilst I myself was fortunate enough to be able to complete my full police service without sustaining serious injury, I came to recognise very quickly just what an important issue Tom's campaign covers, and I will continue to support it in any way that I can.

Kevin Moore BA (Hons); PgD; retired Detective Chief Superintendent, Sussex Police.

AUTHOR'S INTRODUCTION

In the latter part of 2023, I re-started my national campaign to seek medal recognition for the overlooked severely injured on-duty police officers, now extended to include all emergency service personnel.

Since then, I have collated much evidence in support of my proposal including the publishing of my last book 'Dysfunctional Police Family Add Insult To Injury'.

During my journey, I have heard such harrowingly sad stories which have reduced this old copper to tears and anger. I thought it surely could not get worse. Well, I was wrong and wait until you read Gary Pearson's story.

Gary Pearson is a former Greater Manchester Police (GMP) firearms officer. He became one of the members of my Facebook group, 'Campaign for Medal Recognition for Injured UK Police Officers'.

I was absolutely stunned when I heard his story of being shot, causing the loss of an eye and catastrophic facial injuries. Since then, although as yet we have not met, I have found through our many telephone calls that he is one of the bravest, resilient and most personable men I have ever had the pleasure of encountering.

I have Gary's full consent to expose the 40-year scandalous GMP treatment of one of their very own who was so shockingly shot and seriously injured.

CHAPTER 1

NEWS ARTICLE 29 JAN 1991

The following will give the reader a brief outline and insight into the main subject of this book. The article is re-printed here courtesy of the Manchester Evening News:

Exclusive

Secret of cop shot by a Saudi.

By Steve Panter.

Gary Pearson

For seven years the shooting of a Manchester bobby by a Saudi royal bodyguard was covered up.

Today we reveal how the government suppressed the shocking incident to preserve diplomatic relations with the oil-rich Saudis.

Detective Gary Pearson was blasted at point-blank range during a training exercise losing an eye and part of the left side of his face.

The 37-year-old father of two has recently been awarded £45,000 compensation after a series of operations to rebuild his shattered face and fit a glass eye.

After the shooting, a top policeman visited him in hospital and ordered him not to reveal details of the incident. (Gun Scandal Page 7)

Scandal of cop shot by Saudi

The shooting of a Manchester policeman by an Arab royal bodyguard can be exposed for the first time today after a seven-year cover-up.

The officer's eye was shot out in an incident which officially never happened.

Police marksman Gary Pearson's life was saved by a colleague who cradled his head for a 45-minute dash to hospital.

The detective constable was shot at close range with a blank cartridge by a Saudi officer called Mispha during a training exercise in a Northumberland Forest in 1983.

Accident

The incident was accepted as an accident. Gary was ordered to say nothing because if it had become public the Saudi government could have broken off diplomatic relations. But we can reveal he was awarded more than £45,000 compensation after seven years of having his face rebuilt.

At the time of the shooting relations with the Saudis were hanging by a thread after the row two years earlier over a TV documentary Death of a Princess.

Gary was injured as he sat in a van with colleague Det Con Henry Milner after a training session with Arab officers. One of the Saudis pressed a pistol to the driver's window and fired.

The blast took out Gary's eye and Det Con Milner was seriously hurt by flying glass. The Saudi officer dropped the gun in shock.

Det Con Milner despite being badly wounded, insisted on looking after his pal as he was rushed to hospital because of the expertise he gained dealing with injuries while he was a Royal Marine. He cradled Gary and kept him upright to stop him choking.

As Gary recovered, he was visited by an assistant chief constable who told him not to talk about the affair.

After a series of operations to rebuild his face and fit a glass eye, Gary returned to duty. He retired 2 years ago. Now aged 37 he lives in the Prestwich area with his wife and two children.

He still refuses to talk about the incident. "The only other thing I want to say is Henry saved my life," he said. "He kept telling me to hang on. The doctors said I was a fraction of an inch from being a goner."

Loaded

The former GMP officer of 19 years' service, added, "It has had a detrimental effect on my life. But I made up my mind that it was an unfortunate accident and that being bitter would do no good."

His solicitor Aubrey Isaacson said that the Saudi did not realise the gun was loaded with a blank. "When he pulled the trigger, he thought the gun was empty," he said. "It was a dreadful accident."

Det Con Milner, who is still in the firearms unit, recently received the Queen's Police medal for his dedication to duty in risky situations and a long record of charity work.

Today a senior police officer said, "The matter was thoroughly investigated, and it was decided that no further action was necessary."

There was no reply from the Saudi Embassy in London.

After this article appeared, the story remained dormant until I heard it first hand from Gary when he joined my Facebook group in support of the campaign. I decided that with his permission it deserved further coverage and investigation, and this is exactly what I set out to achieve.

CHAPTER 2

GARY'S BRIEF ACCOUNT OF BEING SHOT

The main purpose of my writing this book is to broadcast Gary's sad story, which happily is unique. I also wish to highlight all the issues including the shocking involvement of a foreign national and of the keeping of it under wraps to possibly preserve overseas relationships, if that was the reason for his unsympathetic treatment.

After having whetted the reader's appetite to learn more, you will read further on a more comprehensive account as Gary's story unfolds in chronological order.

Here is a short piece directly from Gary as told by him and in his own words:

'I joined Manchester and Salford police cadets in 1971, later becoming a police constable in 1972.

I've had several encounters with violent criminals, and I have had bones broken and even been hit by a car. I mention this not being big-headed or brag but only to say what I did in the police and to show I gave the job everything.

In 1983 being in firearms, I was seconded to firearms training. I was sent to Kielder Forest with several Saudi police officers to train them in anti-ambush techniques and firearms scenarios.

On November 15, 1983, training having finished for the day, I was sat in the front passenger seat of a personnel carrier when I saw a Saudi officer run from bushes and stand at the driver's window. He raised his .38 revolver to the glass, I heard a loud bang and felt like I'd been punched in the face.

I felt the left-hand side of my face and my fingers went inside my cheek. I knew then it was pretty bad.

I was rushed in the personnel carrier to Carlisle hospital where I was placed on a gurney as I was about to be sent for immediate surgery. My face had swollen so I was unable to see but a nurse came to speak to me. She told me my injuries were serious, and she thought my wife should be with me, but a lockdown had been called for by the police. She said that no one could discuss the circumstances of the shooting, and my wife was not to be told. I gave the nurse my home telephone number and asked her to let my wife know, this she did and so my wife was at least now aware of my injuries.

My wife was then contacted by a senior officer who informed her that I was in the Carlisle hospital and that I had a 'foreign body' in my eye. My wife said she would come up to Carlisle but was told by a senior officer, "Now, now, dear let's not panic. I will keep you informed."

A couple of hours later the same officer rang my wife and said she better go up to Carlisle hospital immediately. My wife was left to travel from Manchester to Carlisle on her own with our 2-year-old son. We were told there was no one available from the police to ferry them to my bedside.

When she got to Carlisle the Scottish police welfare had booked her into a nearby boarding house, GMP welfare could not be contacted.

I stayed in the hospital for a week where they closed the wound as best they could and removed what was left of my left eye and any bone fragments.

When I returned home, I was met with an invoice from GMP welfare asking for the refund of just over £200 which they had paid for my wife and son's week stay in the Carlisle boarding house. Causing some financial difficulty I repaid the monies.

We had just bought our first home; the mortgage was very high, and I was dependent on my wage plus overtime. Now I was on the sick and we were finding it pretty hard to manage financially.

I contacted the head of welfare and told him I was paying into the force's insurance scheme and that it said for the loss of an eye you would get £5000 immediate payout.

He stated it wasn't an immediate payment and that I should either get a loan from a relative or ask my bank for a loan. I told him the advert on the poster near the armoury said 'immediate payouts' and I'd get the details from the notice.

Colleagues and I searched every police station and not one advertisement poster could be found. They had all disappeared.

Throughout all my stay in the hospital and my 2 months at home, I was never visited by police or welfare, not even a phone call, except for the one visit at the hospital by Chief Inspector James on the night of the shooting.

To this day, I do not know why I was shot or what happened to my attacker.

I paid for my face to be rebuilt using titanium plates to replace the lost cheekbone, and my eye socket was repaired using flesh from inside my mouth.

I eventually went back to work but only behind a desk. I spent the next 12-18 months in a fog. I put up with that and being in the office for the next 6 years. It was during this time that a detective inspector first referred to me as 'Cyclops'. I could have either punched him in the face or leave the job I loved, I left.

From being shot to leaving not one senior officer asked how I was or gave me any explanation as to why I had been injured. I was left to get on with it and told to keep my mouth shut.

In about 1990, I took GMP to court for compensation. They wouldn't even agree the Saudis were in the country but eventually I did receive an out-of-court settlement.'

AUTHOR'S COMMENT

Have you ever heard a more shocking uncaring story than this? If anyone still believes there is such a mythical beast as a 'Police Family' then this is surely testament that it is nothing more than mere propaganda. Would a member of any genuine family refer to a loved one who had lost an eye as 'Cyclops?' Phew!

Must we really believe there was no one at all within police circles to drive Gary's wife the 220 miles to Carlisle to be at the bedside of one of their very own who possibly may not survive?

If those on duty were ALL committed duty wise, which is unlikely, and there was this so-called 'Police Family' then surely someone would have volunteered for the driving job during their own free time?

If a real family showed similar neglect the police would be calling for social services and a public enquiry.

Gary's full story will continue later.

CHAPTER 3

INJURED ON-DUTY OFFICERS

There are far too many other brave officers who were also treated badly, and their health and job sacrifice have never been recognised with a medal. The reason being is that there are other medal awards already available but only for gallantry. However, there is nothing for injury without the added gallantry. With the bar set so high for the necessary criteria for gallantry medals, these are only rarely awarded.

Most officers are deprived of an opportunity to show gallantry because they are attacked instantly and without warning or sustain an injury in another way. That is where the problem lies and why so many killed and injured officers in the past 200 years have received no medal recognition whatsoever.

On 9 March 2024, the national disgrace of the overlooking was partially corrected by the introduction of the posthumous Elizabeth Emblem, meaning that the next of kin of all public servants who were killed on duty and sadly will be in the future and backdated to 1948 will be eligible for the award.

However, the flaw is the surviving injured are once again overlooked, hence the important need to adopt my campaign proposal.

My proposal is mainly directed towards, but not solely for, those officers who were deprived ONLY by the injury of reaching the eligibility period for the 'Long Service & Good Conduct Medal', i.e. 20 years but before 2010 it was 22 years but reduced to 20 in line with the armed forces.

To be absolutely clear my proposal is in no way for a medal for bravery, heroism or gallantry BUT merely to recognise the health and job sacrifice of the injured.

Gary's uncaring treatment is not entirely unique, but I have to say it is by far the most shocking extreme example I have ever heard.

He makes the strong point that he does not believe he is the only one who was injured and treated badly. He therefore adamantly insists that a good portion of this book includes a number of accounts gathered from others who were also injured on duty and treated shabbily by their force.

His reasons for demanding the inclusions are because he wants to highlight the enormity of the problem of those injured, their poor treatment and the long-term impact on many affected. In addition, he wishes to broadcast the need to recognise the sacrifices of those affected in order to boost interest and support for the ongoing campaign.

These reasons are what motivates Gary to tell his story and not to seek sympathy or any other self-promotion purpose. He would of course ultimately wish to know the truth behind his shooting. However, he says if the telling of what happened to him only assists in bringing about much needed added attention and a boost for the campaign, then he will be satisfied.

This is typical of the selfless Gary's caring and gracious nature and one I shall therefore honour.

So, although my initial intention was to focus solely on documenting Gary's tragic story, in compliance with his wishes, indeed demands, here follows more shocking examples obtained directly from the overlooked and forgotten injured which I submit proves the urgency for my proposed new medal.

Gary's story will continue after these accounts.

PC DAVID RATHBAND (Late)

PC David Rathband,

as he recovers in hospital, with his twin brother, Darren.

On July 3, 2010, only 2 days after being released from Durham prison, 37-year-old Northumbrian, Raul Moat shot and wounded his ex-girlfriend Samantha Stobbart, 22, with a sawn-off shotgun and killed her new boyfriend Chris Brown, 29.

Samantha had wrongly told Moat that Chris was a serving police officer because she quite rightly feared reprisals for dumping him.

Rather than having the desired effect of deterring Moat from seeking revenge it further enraged his hatred for the police. Tree surgeon and club bouncer Moat had in the past sought psychiatric help.

The following day, Moat phoned 999 to 'declare war' on the police.

About 10 minutes later, close to East Denton, Moat then shot and blinded PC David Rathband as he sat in his parked patrol car on the outskirts of Newcastle.

Moat then went on the run sparking a nationwide manhunt seeking to capture him. He fled to the quiet village of Rothbury, Northumberland with the help of two accomplices and was eventually tracked down camping out in a rural area that he knew well.

7 days after the shootings and surrounded by armed police, 2 stun guns were fired in the hope of subduing him, but he turned the shotgun on himself and was killed.

PC Rathband had suffered catastrophic injuries including the loss of his sight. In the following months, he battled with his appalling injuries, and he inspired the nation with his determination to return to the job he loved.

After the shooting, David explained, "I looked into his eyes and saw nothing - no emotion. Then I felt the pain full-on in my face. I knew my right eye socket had just exploded and my eye had gone."

His 20-year marriage to his wife, Kath, failed and the couple separated. They had a son and a daughter together.

In February 2012, 2 days after returning from visiting his twin brother, Darren, also a police officer, in Australia, sadly David succumbed to his understandable depression, and he took his own life at his home in Blyth.

He had set up a charity to help other stricken emergency services personnel and went on to win a Daily Mirror Pride of Britain award for his bravery at a celebrity-packed ceremony.

He wrote his own autobiography and spent huge amounts of time fundraising and making public appearances after setting up the Blue Lamp Foundation, which still exists today.

DARREN RATHBAND'S QUOTE

Here is an eloquent and helpful quote from Darren which he says can be used in any media broadcast:

'Since the inception of the police service and the other emergency services men and women who are injured whilst carrying out their duties, have been forgotten.

It is time that those who are injured are given the recognition of their sacrifice in service.

Awarding a medal to injured police and emergency workers serves multiple important purposes:

1. *Recognition of Sacrifice*: A medal symbolises acknowledgment of the sacrifices made by these individuals in the line of duty. It honours their commitment to protecting and serving the community, often at great personal risk.

2. *Moral Support*: Receiving a medal can provide emotional validation to injured workers. It serves as a reminder that their hard work and

sacrifices are appreciated, fostering a sense of pride and belonging in their profession.

3. *Inspiration for Others*: Medals can act as powerful symbols that inspire current and future generations of first responders. They highlight the values of courage, service, and resilience, encouraging others to follow in their footsteps.

4. *Community Gratitude*: Awarding medals publicly shows the community's appreciation and respect for the sacrifices made by these heroes. It strengthens community ties and reinforces the importance of support for those who serve and protect.

5. *Promotion of a Culture of Valour*: By formally recognising injured workers, it promotes a culture that values bravery, dedication, and commitment. This culture can boost morale within emergency services and encourage teamwork and excellence among colleagues.

6. *Legacy of Service*: Medals serve as a lasting memento of an individual's contributions, memorialising their story and ensuring that their service and sacrifice are remembered over time.

Overall, awarding a medal is a meaningful gesture that encapsulates gratitude, respect, and recognition for the profound impacts these individuals have on their communities.

A small token and recognition of those who deserve to be honoured.

Not all officers who are injured have the opportunity to be called heroes or show a level of gallantry to be considered for the only police medal available for those who are unfortunate to sustain injuries on duty like my late brother PC David Rathband.

Their sacrifice and legacy of service is marked by only the scars of those injuries.

Their injuries in service must be recognised and they should be honoured by the government and community they gave so much for.'

Darren Rathband

AUTHOR'S COMMENT

The campaign is now jointly dedicated to the memory of both PC David Rathband and John Hadfield, also a former police officer injured on duty. Sadly, both are no longer with us.

Neither David nor John received any medal recognition whatsoever for their health sacrifice or to show even a connection to the police service.

I am privileged to have David's twin brother Darren with me to offer his full support for my campaign.

RIP David and John.

John's story follows on from David's.

JOHN HADFIELD (Late)

John Hadfield (Late)

The following article is produced courtesy of the Dorset Echo, 21 March 2024.

'A former officer for Dorset Police, who was stabbed in the line of duty, hopes fellow officers who have been severely injured will receive an official government award.

John Hadfield, 74, is supporting a campaign set up by retired Sussex police officer Thomas Curry to ensure that officers, who are injured on duty and then medically discharged, receive a government award in recognition of their service.

On March 9, the government announced police, firefighters and other service workers who died in the line of duty would receive The Elizabeth Emblem – a posthumous award for their service.

A second campaign was set up due to concerns that those who were severely injured and medically discharged were "overlooked and forgotten".

Mr Hadfield has recently been diagnosed with terminal cancer and hopes other servicemen, if not himself, will be able to finally receive national recognition for their health sacrifices.

"I might not know whether the campaign will be successful, I might not live long enough to receive this award but it's important servicemen are recognised for the health sacrifices they have made."

After spending many years in the army, Mr Hadfield began working for Dorset Police in Bridport, Dorchester, and Weymouth for ten years before being transferred to the Regional Crime Squad in Bristol in 1986.

In December 1990, while arresting a male for an attempted burglary in Bristol city centre, Mr Hadfield was stabbed five times.

He said: "I was very lucky that I was only half a mile from the Royal Infirmary. They saved my life as one of the stab wounds nicked my aorta, so I was bleeding to death.

"I'm so grateful for that. It's the things that came afterwards that affected me. I had to walk past where I got stabbed as that was where I worked, it was quite macabre."

Mr Hadfield was medically discharged in July 1994 after 19 years and 10 months of service.

He developed Post-Traumatic Stress Disorder (PTSD) since the incident and has previously done charity work, supporting Combat Stress and The Household Cavalry Foundation - charities that support veterans with mental health and PTSD.

He received no service medals as the initial criterion for the police 'Long Service and Good Conduct Medal' was 22 years' service.

"I didn't get a medal, through no fault of my own, and a lot of police officers are in the same situation as me who had a lot more serious injuries that will follow them through the rest of their lives. There was no recognition at all for what you did if you hadn't done 22 years."

Thomas Curry launched a campaign in late September calling for a new service medal to be bestowed on officers who have been injured during their work then medically discharged. His parliament petition currently has 3,465 signations with over 1,000 members on their Facebook page.

"This is a national 200-year-old scandal of overlooking those affected and harrowingly sad stories have come to me from all over the U.K. including that of John Hadfield."

"This is particularly sad because he has terminal cancer and doesn't know how much more time he has. John has said that he would dearly love to see this be approved during his lifetime."'

AUTHOR'S COMMENT

I am in awe of John's bravery both whilst he served as a police officer and up to his dignified passing. Sadly, as he predicted, he did not live long enough to see the campaign succeed or to receive his long overdue recognition.

The campaign is dedicated to John and PC David Rathband's memory.

I truly hope they are both looking down on us, from their rightful place above, when the campaign proposal is finally approved.

PAM WHITE

Pam White

'I joined the Metropolitan Police Service in September 1980. I really enjoyed my job and was in line to take my sergeant's exams. However, everything changed on 17th December 1983.

I was on uniform duty in King's Road, Chelsea and responded together with other colleagues to a possible bomb threat either inside or outside Harrods.

The IRA gave about a 30-minute warning but we frontline troops on the ground were not informed it was a coded message.

I arrived at Harrods about 10 minutes after the call and there met up with a few other colleagues who were also in attendance. We sealed off the one-way street and we were busily engaged in searching under and around parked cars and assisting members of the public to safety.

I spoke to a colleague, Jane Arbuthnot, and had just turned my back when a car parked next to us exploded. It contained 30lbs of Semtex provided by Libya. The blast lifted me off my feet and tragically Jane was killed outright. I later learnt 3 civilians died at the scene along with Sergeant Noel Lane and my inspector, Stephen Dodd, who died a week later. 13 other colleagues were injured at the scene.

I and other officers continued to guide the public to safety, and we stayed so engaged until later when we were told we could stand down. I also gave first aid even though I was in shock myself. We were informed another bomb was going off and that was very scary to say the least.

To cut a long story short my career ended that day. I was put on restricted duties suffered health issues and still do today 40 years on. I was given a medical discharge from the police service in July 86 because of my injuries and not being able to fulfil my duties. I had no choice in the matter.

We had no debriefing etc. and I became very ill. I was admitted to the medical centre at Hendon from Feb to August 84, and on discharge was then forced to change stations.

I was shocked to find later that I was ostracised by many colleagues who because they could not see my injuries, said I was making it up to gain attention. That was very hard to deal with indeed.

I was very sad to leave the police, a job I loved, and I struggled to find employment after my forced early medical retirement. Fortunately, I survived.

I do strongly feel that officers like me who lose their health and career should be awarded recognition for their loss and bravery.

I spoke to various senior officers at the Met. about this, but it went no further than that.'

AUTHOR'S COMMENT

Pam's sacrifice also remains unrecognised and for over 40 years.

What truly adds 'insult to injury' is that whilst the long-overdue posthumous recognition, the Elizabeth Emblem, was finally approved on 9 March 2024 once again the injured are overlooked and forgotten.

How can it ever be acceptable for Pam to witness her killed colleagues, quite rightly, recognised with the award (albeit after 40 shameful overlooking years) but because she miraculously survived but sustained a life-changing injury and sacrificed her job, as a direct result of the same incident and her actions were identical, she and others are ignored.

This is why the campaign is so necessary and must succeed to correct the national disgrace and as soon as possible!

HARRODS' BOMB

To assist readers who may be unfamiliar with the bombing incident referred to by Pam, I am including a short summary here:

On the afternoon of 17 December 1983, IRA members parked a car containing a bomb near the side entrance of Harrods, on Hans Crescent,

London.

The bomb exploded at about 13:21, as four police officers in a car, an officer on foot and a police dog handler neared the suspect vehicle.

Six people were killed (three officers and three bystanders) and 90 others were injured, including 9 children and 14 police officers.

The blast damaged 24 cars and all five floors on the side of Harrods. The police car absorbed much of the blast and this likely prevented further casualties.

The huge impact ripped through Hans Crescent, which was crowded with Christmas shoppers. A warning had been received but the bomb device exploded as the police were attempting to clear the area. The next day the IRA admitted to placing the car bomb and a few days later they expressed their 'regret' saying that the operation had not been authorised.

Harrods shop windows were blown out causing severe injuries to staff and customers. Despite the damage, the store re-opened three days later, vowing not to be defeated by acts of terrorism.

In 1984 the Police Memorial Trust was set up to erect memorials to those officers killed on duty at or near the place where they fell. The film director and Kensington resident, the late Sir Michael Winner, was the founder of the charitable trust which is run from an office in Kensington High Street.

One of the first memorials to be erected was to those killed by the IRA bomb in 1983. Princess Alexandra performed the unveiling on 24 September 1985. Lord Whitelaw represented the Government and gave a short speech.

The families of Inspector Stephen Dodd, Police Sergeant Noel Lane and Woman Police Constable Jane Arbuthnot all attended the ceremony.

Margaret Thatcher, then prime minister, and Neil Kinnock, then leader of the opposition, attended later to pay their respects and lay flowers.

The Royal Borough of Kensington and Chelsea later commissioned a similar tablet in remembrance of the three innocent civilians who died - Philip Gededes, Kenneth Gerald Salvesen and Jasmine Cochran Patrick - which was placed immediately above the memorial to the police officers.

There were no medals awarded to any of the killed or injured for what they suffered that sad day.

Over 40 years later, on 9 March 2024, the posthumous Elizabeth Emblem finally recognises those killed but sadly to date, there remains no recognition for the severely injured.

Hopefully, that will soon be corrected with the success of the campaign.

SIMON BYWATER

Simon Bywater

'I returned home from the chaos of a war zone, having witnessed the trauma and misery of conflict in northern Iraq, as a Royal Marine. The transition back to normal life was jarring, with no debriefing or support to help process what I had experienced. While the familiar sights of England brought some relief, the lack of decompression left me to silently carry the weight of what I'd seen. With little opportunity to talk about the horrors of war, I brushed off questions with simple responses, choosing to focus on the future while the memories of the battlefield faded into the background.

Within weeks I had joined Greater Manchester Police, and the year was 1991. I was surprised by how laid-back Greater Manchester Police (GMP) training felt compared to the strict discipline of the Royal Marines. Expecting tough training, I instead found a system focused on self-assessments and character analysis that seemed more intent on highlighting weaknesses.

Adjusting to civilian life was challenging, especially working with a mixed group of people, where I had to be cautious about offending anyone. The law felt confusing, and long classroom sessions often bored me. Once posted to Brownley Road Police Station in Wythenshawe and out on the streets, I began to feel more at ease, using common sense and practical skills to handle real-world issues. Although the police codes of practice were meant to help, I often felt it hindered effective crime-fighting.

I had two tutor constables: Stan, a tough, no-nonsense cop, and Jim, who approached problems thoughtfully and offered me a valuable piece of advice: "If you start to hate the job, get out because it'll make your life miserable."

My fitness from the Marines served me well, especially when facing violent confrontations, but the trauma began to take its toll. The violence I witnessed daily began to affect me deeply, though like many officers of the time I pushed through, trying to switch off after long shifts. The birth of my daughter shifted my perspective on the darker side of society, as I realised its potential impact on her life.

After facing numerous violent incidents, including an attack that shattered my nose and teeth, I persevered but felt my confidence waver. I continued working in challenging conditions, joined the divisional crime squad, and took on dangerous work targeting drug dealers and recovering firearms. Despite my professional success, the internal pressure and lack of support slowly wore me down. Court cases, with their legal games, only added to my disillusionment. Public perception of police officers made it hard to unwind and began to avoid social interactions, feeling labelled and misunderstood.

A tragic night during a routine call changed everything. I found myself trying to save the life of a young army corporal who had been stabbed. The trauma of watching the man die in my arms was overwhelming, but there was no time to process it. I was back at work within hours, giving evidence in court, and felt as if no one, particularly my supervisory officers, understood or cared about the mental toll the work was taking on me.

Though I continued my work, my growing frustration with the police system only deepened. Despite becoming a detective, handling high-profile cases, and facing relentless violent crime in areas like Moss Side, the overwhelming stress of the job and the trauma I carried with me remained. I realised that no amount of professional success could erase the psychological damage I had endured. Attempts to suppress the memories failed, and eventually, I reached a breaking point. Transferring to a quieter police force in Cambridgeshire didn't provide the relief I had hoped for, as flashbacks and trauma continued to haunt me.

In the end, I recognised that the violence and trauma I faced in GMP were as severe, if not worse than some of my experiences in a war zone. Yet, the support for officers like me was severely lacking, leaving me and many others to bear the psychological toll of policing without help. Looking back, my experience reflects a broader failure to provide essential support for those serving on the front lines of policing in GMP at the time.

I faced numerous violent situations during my time with Greater Manchester Police (GMP), including witnessing the murder of a soldier. Despite the traumatic nature of these incidents, GMP never offered me any form of counselling or mental health support. When I eventually transferred to another force, GMP neither inquired about my reasons for leaving nor provided me with any evidence of service, reflecting a complete lack of follow-up or care for my well-being.

Upon transferring to Cambridgeshire, I found little improvement in my mental health. Eventually, I had to accept that I could no longer continue, and I was medically discharged with a diagnosis of severe, complex PTSD. I was devastated by this outcome, and with no support from the police, it took me many years to find purpose within myself again.

Although I hold a General Service Medal from my time in the Royal Marines, I received no recognition from the police service. This lack of acknowledgement feels like a sombre reflection of how the service regards me, and so many others, who were forced to retire due to medical injuries.'

AUTHOR'S COMMENT

Veteran Royal Marine, Simon's story highlights the fact that anyone can be affected by the toll police work can take on one's mental health.

Only in modern times PTSD and similar complaints have begun to be recognised but such recognition and care still have a way to go. We must remember that only a little over 100 years ago, during WW1, brave young soldiers, showing the same symptoms, were accused of cowardice and 'shot at dawn'. Privately, some retain a non-sensical belief that there is a connotation but that thinking too should be confined to history.

An injury as far as being injured on duty is concerned is defined as being 'any injury of body or mind'. Therefore, Simon and others are equally entitled to my medal proposal in exactly the same way as those who sustained a physical injury.

Simon served with the Royal Marines from Sept. 85 to Oct.1991. He then served with Greater Manchester Police from Oct. 1991 to 1999 and then he transferred to Cambridgeshire Constabulary until 2000.

SUE MITCHELL

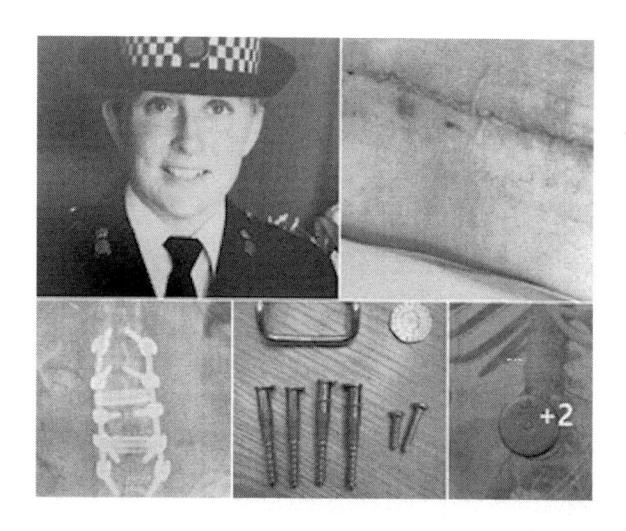

Sue Mitchell

'Firstly, before I introduce myself, I would like to thank Tom Curry for all his dedication and hard work fighting for us all, with his campaign.

From a very young child all I wanted to do was be a police officer. I'm quite sure I got the idea from watching Dixon of Dock Green. I was fascinated with the police work and the excitement they all had on a daily basis. Those feelings of wanting to join the police never left me and as I grew so did the longing to be a policewoman.

I am now 62 but I can clearly recall that to achieve my ambition to be a policewoman, I never gave up applying to join and after 8 years and returning to college to improve my qualifications I was finally accepted and joined the Essex Police in 1984 at the age of 22.

After completing my 14 weeks' training, unfortunately on my 5th day of duty after a car chase, I was run down by a robbers' getaway vehicle. They tried to drive right over me, and I received many injuries including a fractured knee, hand and worse of all to my spine.

After 6 months I was able to return to duty as I was desperate to get back on with my career, but I continued to suffer from the spinal injuries. Sadly, my force had other ideas and put me under pressure to resign which I refused to do. I would always be put out on the beat day and night. I never complained or gave up, so they extended my probation to 4 years.

I was so worried and desperate to continue with my career that I requested a meeting with the chief constable (CC) to explain just how important it was to me. On the day, I didn't get to see the CC and I was surprisingly put in front of the assistant CC. He had no compassion whatsoever and his words to me were, "Why should I keep you in my force, when I can have someone who is 100% fit?"

I continued to suffer spinal problems and in 1987 it was discovered that I required, what was to be the first of 16 major spinal surgeries. The first surgery was carried out privately in November 1987.

On 20th December 1987, I returned home in a body plaster cast and 3 days later the force welfare officer visited me at home to inform me I was going to be medically retired. That is when the bottom fell out of my world.

Since the accident I have undergone a total of 26 major surgeries, and I have a morphine pump implanted in my abdomen to help control the spinal pain. I now have a spine full of metalwork.

I have also spent 8 weeks in a mental hospital (a Victorian asylum full of cockroaches) after suffering a breakdown in 1990. The force never even bothered to send welfare to visit me to see how I was coping. They just ignored it completely. I now suffer heart problems and have suffered 3 strokes. I have spent £150,000 of my own finances on private medical treatment and surgeries.

Until I found out about Tom's other book, 'Dysfunctional Police Family Add Insult To Injury' and his Facebook group, I honestly thought I was the only officer to have been treated in such a shabby way. I now know this is not the case and I realise now that there are so many of us who have given our loyal service, been injured in our job within the police and then been merely cast aside and left to just suffer alone.

I haven't heard from my force since 1988 when I retired. I have to agree with Tom, there is no 'police family' and the fact we are all cast aside and forgotten does add insult to injury.

Just to make matters worse for me, whilst the TV and press were involved, senior officers told how I would receive a 'commendation' for my bravery as I caught one of the robbers. Well, I am still waiting for it, it never arrived! It just may have made me feel a little better about the loss of my career should I have received it!

Fat was thrown on the fire of pain, while I was waiting to be medically retired. My sergeant and the newest probationer/bag carrier on my shift turned up unannounced at my home one evening, shortly after I had been discharged from the hospital to recover from my very first of many spinal surgeries.

I thought the visit was a welfare check but much to my horror they had come to collect my uniform. It was a complete shock and something I have never gotten over considering I had done nothing wrong, except get run over by robbers in the course of my duties.

The worst insult was when the sergeant asked me to remove all the police insignia from my uniforms before putting them into the black plastic rubbish sacks they had provided. I refused to do this and just handed them my uniforms as I was so horrified and hurt.

I'm sure I do suffer from PTSD. I have never been assessed, neither have I mentioned the psychological problems I have continued to suffer for all these years, added to, by that hurtful evening my sergeant arrived.

Some of you may remember the old American TV programme 'Branded'. The series was set in the Old West, following the end of the American Civil War. The show starred Chuck Connors as Jason McCord, a United States Army Cavalry captain who had been court-martialled and drummed out of the service following an unjust accusation of cowardice.

The programme starts with the army captain standing in his uniform when a senior officer removes his hat, his army insignia, belt and sword and banishes him from the fort.

I thought I would mention this clip as it sums up my feelings of how I was made to feel the evening my sergeant and the probationer arrived to remove my uniforms.

For me, it has been a long unhappy 40 years of pain and heartbreak. I just wish I had known all I know now about the unhappiness, unpleasantness and hurt a career in the police service can bring if injured.

I used to think I was alone in the terrible way I was treated by the police and the Home Office after my accident. Now I know there are many other police officers who have been injured and received similar shocking treatment.

That is why I fully support Tom Curry's 'Campaign for Medal Recognition for Police and Emergency Services'. Hopefully, the campaign may help to halt any further injured police officers and emergency personnel from receiving the overlooking and bad treatment so many of us have already endured.'

AUTHOR'S COMMENT

This is yet another harrowing tale and the sad end to a young woman's police career which she had always wanted. A tragic story of one more dispensable officer who was cast aside and forgotten once, so severely, injured and no longer of any value to the police service.

The 'Branded' TV clip is uncannily so appropriate, but the main difference is that WPC Sue Mitchell was not accused of cowardice but had acted so bravely only to receive such catastrophic life changing injuries. However, her uniform was also ordered to be stripped of its insignia, and she too was discharged from the service.

Sue's sacrifice will continue to be unrecognised until the campaign succeeds and gains the King's approval.

ANDREW HUTCHISON

Andrew Hutchison

'I joined GMP on the 29th of April 1991, having been a member of a Roman Catholic religious order since 1976.

I spent the next five years serving as a police officer, being promoted to sergeant after three and a half years of service, whilst at the same time still being an active member of the Order.

The day I joined I was given the nickname 'Rasputin: the mad monk'. That name stayed with me throughout my service.

At 02.19hrs on Tuesday 10th February 2006, I was in uniform and on mobile patrol in Littleborough, Rochdale. I was stationary in my signed police vehicle with my blue lights flashing when my police vehicle was struck head-on, at 70mph, by a male driving a stolen motor vehicle.

The 22-year-old male driver of the stolen car had in his pocket a suicide letter addressed to his 16-year-old girlfriend. Within the letter, the offender describes to his girlfriend how he intends to commit suicide by driving head-on into something - that something was my marked police vehicle. The male had a dislike of police officers and decided to kill himself by means of 'suicide by cop'. A method of suicide in which you kill yourself and a police officer at the same time.

Both the offender and I survived. Although initially arrested for attempted murder he was later charged with dangerous driving and given a two-year sentence of which he served eight months.

In 2006 it was, unlike now, unusual to use a vehicle as a weapon, therefore the CPS refused to charge this offender with either attempted murder or grievous bodily harm.

He sustained serious injuries. I survived due to the protection offered by my body armour which absorbed most of the impact. However, I also sustained serious head and spinal injuries which required surgery and have been left with a traumatic brain injury for which I still take medication. I still suffer from PTSD and my life has been altered completely as a result of this incident.

I had never previously met or spoken to this offender. He did not know me. He hit my vehicle simply as a result of a domestic he had with his girlfriend which led him to decide to commit suicide.

My personality changed as a result of this head injury, and I am no longer the same person I once was. This attack left me with chronic pain and I had to take medical retirement in 2010 as a direct result of the injuries I received. I still suffer as a consequence of this incident to this day.

I left the police service with four commendations, including two for bravery, one of which is a Judge's Commendation.

My two-year probationary period was difficult as some colleagues did not like the idea of a man who had previously been a Roman Catholic priest serving as an officer. They thought it their duty to make life as difficult for me as possible, sad but true. Fortunately, most colleagues regarded me as just that, a colleague.

I felt that I was a happy person, but the injury changed all that.

Initially, I was off work for four months recovering from the assault. The greater injury however was to my brain. My personality changed. I would become explosive for no reason. My neurosurgeon told me that my brain had smashed against the back of my skull at 70mph and then forward damaging the frontal lobe.

I now suffer from irritability, mood swings, short-term memory loss, and a sense of aggression. Inside I felt like 'The Incredible Hulk'. It was as if some green creature lived inside my head and the 'old Andrew' could not compete with the 'new Andrew'. I felt as if the 'old Andrew' had died in that collision and this 'thing' that looked and talked like me was all that remained. Additionally, I lost about 50% of power in my right arm.

The chronic pain was difficult to deal with. I was prescribed 20 strong pain-killing tablets a day as well as Ora Morph as a backup. Naturally, 18 years of all that medication has brought additional problems.

My faith took a battering, and my consultant informed me my brain no longer produces serotonin. All in all, each day feels like a personal battle. I now feel after 18 years that I can manage most of the issues I suffer from by taking all necessary steps to avoid the trigger points.

People see me and do not see any visible injuries and think I must be okay. They have no idea of the personal struggle each day brings.'

AUTHOR'S COMMENT

Andrew is indisputably a good man, but he still suffered mockery for his faith and beliefs and shockingly from those within police circles.

At sentencing the first thing the judge asked was, "Why has this man not been charged with an offence against the person?"

It's little wonder the soft sentence was so disproportionate to the crime because the judge was restricted and clearly from his opening comment, he too thought a more serious and appropriate charge should have been laid.

The CPS agent had not seen the file until twenty minutes before sentencing.

Why the CPS chose not to charge attempted murder is beyond my comprehension, given that the evidence was there to support the charge i.e. the suicide note detailing the intention to commit 'suicide by cop', as quoted by Andrew.

Andrew was the innocent victim of a callous 'cop hater' and as a result of the attack continues to suffer the catastrophic physical consequences daily.

TRACY MATHER

Tracy Mather

'Since being a child, I had always wanted to be a policewoman and to serve in the police. I eventually achieved my ambition when I joined the Greater Manchester Police in 1979.

In 1980 I was assaulted by a young male who was wearing steel-toe-capped boots. I was going to the assistance of another PC who I saw attacked by the male who kicked him breaking his leg.

As I ran towards the youth he turned and kicked me in between the legs and the force of the kick took me off my feet. I was able to continue and apprehend the male and placed him in the back of the van as other officers arrived.

At this point, I passed out from the pain in my lower area. I came round in hospital where I was examined and was told that the kick had caused bruising to my vagina and cervix. I had pain in my lower back and hips.

I was informed after a few years that I would probably be able to get pregnant but unable to carry to full term. However, I did successfully give birth to 3 children but sadly lost 3 on the way.

After ten years of pain and my right leg just giving out from under me it was discovered that one of the nerves that run from the spine and around your pelvis was actually trapped in the hip socket. I had an operation to rectify it, but I was still in pain.

Over the years I have been in different degrees of pain, but it is there 24/7. The 3 discs at the top and bottom of my spine have welded together making it difficult to walk or bend and each movement causes a grinding sensation in both areas.

I received no care or welfare from the police on being injured and felt abandoned. I continued to serve until 1989 when I was medically discharged. I received no recognition of my health or job sacrifice.'

AUTHOR'S COMMENT

Courageous Tracy has suffered much after losing the job she longed for since childhood. Her pain and disability continue to impact on her life.

She is another prime candidate for my medal proposal.

ANDY WALKER

Andy Walker

'I was on night duty in August 1998, crewed with a female officer and we were the mobile patrol covering the sub-divisions of Hazel Grove, Adswood, Cheadle Hulme within the Greater Manchester Police (GMP) area.

An abandoned call 999 had been received from a female involved in a violent domestic. I was driving and so with blue lights and sirens, we made haste to the address. It was nearly midnight, and it had been raining but had stopped and the road was wet.

I approached a junction with the main A6 in Stockport, this junction was staggered from left to right. A car attempted to go straight across the A6 and appeared right in front of me. We collided with the vehicle and the next thing I knew was that the car had gone, and the front of my vehicle was badly damaged. I had impacted the passenger side of the other vehicle.

I recall seeing smoke from the front of my vehicle and then from the corner of my eye, I saw the female officer, in the front seat, moving. I remember then switching the lights and sirens off and the ignition too. That was it and I blacked out.

I was taken to the hospital where I was put on morphine for the pain. I had damaged my lower spine and apparently, my heart was swollen. I was then off work from that day and never returned.

Due to my injuries and PTSD, I couldn't go near a car without panicking. The force doctor in GMP made several visits to my home.

On his last visit in May 1999, he informed me he was returning me unfit for duty as I wouldn't be able to do frontline duties again. This came as a shock to me because I was only off work for 9 months at this time. Anyway, he said he would leave me to think about it and any questions to contact him the next day.

I talked it over that evening with my then-wife and I decided that I did have a few questions for the doctor. At the time I was fully trained in communications and on all the computers and I thought I could be still kept on in some capacity.

I contacted him the following day and before I had a chance to speak and explain my thoughts as to how I may be redeployed, he said, "It's OK I have done and signed all the paperwork, and your finishing date is 17th June 1999."

Well, that was that, nothing from the federation at any point no contact whatsoever not even from the divisional representative and when I contacted them, I was told to wait for a package from police personnel and sign what was needed. I did that and sent it back. So that it and my 20 1/2 years of service, including 2 years as a cadet, finished.

After the accident, I needed counselling and help to get back to driving and this took several months as I was unable to stand near a vehicle at first never mind get in one and drive it.

The officer in the accident case arranged for me to receive additional counselling to try and get me to recall the incident because due to the trauma my brain had blocked it all out. Apparently, this is common in such serious cases.

During this time, it became clear I did see the front seat passenger's arm, in the other car, hanging out of the vehicle. I was later told she had passed away at the scene on impact.

My female colleague had whiplash, but I believe because of PTSD she too never returned to police duty.

The driver of the offending car had cuts and bruises. He was found to be 3 1/2 times over the legal drink driving limit. He was subsequently sentenced to 8 1/2 years imprisonment as it was his 3rd drunk driving offence and also the vehicle was not his and he had no insurance.

When the dust settled the only contact I had was from a divisional inspector, who came to my home to collect what uniform I had and my warrant card.

That was the sad end to my career, and I have no medal recognition to show any connection to the police service.

I joined the GMP police cadets in July 1978 and then became a police constable in July 1980. I was medically retired on 18 June 1999.'

ANONYMOUS GMP FEMALE SERVING OFFICER

'A Greater Manchester Police 30-year-old female officer attended a domestic dispute in 2005. A male occupant at the address, under the influence of drink and drugs and out of control, deliberately kicked an external front door glass panel completely shattering the glass.

Unfortunately, the policewoman was standing close to the door and a shard of glass struck her in the eye. She was rushed to the hospital but sadly the eye was irreparable, and it was lost. The policewoman, nearly 20 years later, continues to serve in Greater Manchester Police. In two years' time she is due to retire having courageously completed a full 30 years of service. Whilst she will leave with her 'Long Service & Good Conduct Medal' she will have nothing in recognition of her health sacrifice.'

AUTHOR'S COMMENT

I am in complete awe of her dedication to duty and determination to carry on serving the public. Understandably she wishes her full identity to remain anonymous.

I wish the brave lady a happy soon fully earned retirement.

JOHN O'ROURKE

John O'Rourke

'I joined Greater Manchester Police (GMP), as a cadet in June 1979 and the following year in August 1980, became a police constable in GMP.

Following training at Bruche Police Training Centre in Warrington, I was posted to the D Division, one of the city divisions within GMP. A great area to learn to police, busy and diverse.

During this time, I performed foot patrol duties including, panda and van duties. I was injured several times in the execution of my duties. Some injuries were as a result of criminal assault and others whilst making arrests where injuries were sustained. These occurrences were common among operational officers. It was accepted (possibly, naively), that operational officers will face violent situations and will need to act accordingly, which understandably can result in injury to the officer. A risk we were prepared to take, keeping the streets safe for the public to go about their business knowing that the police were looking after them.

In 1985 I was an aide with the CID. On 29th June 1985 along with a detective we went to an address in the Longsight area to interview a suspect in relation to a burglary. He denied his true identity, produced a 7.65mm unique self-loading pistol and tried to make good his escape. A foot pursuit ensued where he carefully took aim with the pistol at me and tried to discharge it on 3 separate occasions. I closed on him, and I was able to disarm him but during the struggle, he produced a 14" screwdriver and attempted to stab me in the abdomen. I deflected the blow with my right hand, which resulted in an injury to my right hand and a minor injury to my abdomen.

With the aid of my colleague, the male was subdued and arrested and for this action, I was awarded, 'The Queen's Commendation for Bravery'.

I returned to uniform duties, which I found a great pleasure, apart from again during this period, I was assaulted on many occasions, in the execution of my duties.

In the following years, I performed duties in the Tactical Aid Group (TAG), firearms at Manchester Airport and subsequently returned to mainstream policing.

In 1998, I joined the Tactical Vehicle Crime Unit (TVCU), which was involved in intelligence led operations targeting organised gangs that stole high-powered cars to perform ram raids and armed robberies. I also qualified as a VIP driver and this consisted of Category 'A' prisoner escort duties, royal visits, driving VIPs, witness protection and assisting section officers and divisions with major local issues.

During my time with TVCU, I was rammed on several occasions by stolen cars, attempting to make good their escape. Once again, these resulted in further injuries to me.

In June 1999 I was injured again when a suspect deliberately rammed my police vehicle, hitting my police car so hard, that the front nearside wheel buckled. I was badly jolted by the force of the impact. I received an injury to my left shoulder and damage to my neck, resulting in my having to report sick. I was treated for whiplash and had extensive physiotherapy on my shoulder and neck. Against advice, I returned to work still carrying these injuries.

I feared that the force medical officer (FMO) who wanted to see me would end my career, as other officers with lengthy service seemed to be pensioned off. I did not want this. The inevitable happened and one evening I was summoned to see one of the FMOs. He showed concern with my left shoulder and was about to write something down on paper. I stopped him momentarily as I noted the watch he was wearing, a particular military watch. We chatted about the forces, and he asked me a question, "Are you fit for operational duties?" I replied, "Yes." He told me that he was not happy with my left shoulder and wanted to examine me again in 3 months. Reprieve I thought.

I returned to my duties but never made it to the 3 months as I was once again involved in a violent ramming and received further injuries to my left shoulder and neck.

As a result, I was informed that my injuries now prevented me from continuing as a police officer. I felt totally flat, deflated and almost useless, as all my hard work and devotion to duty was being taken away just like that.

I was medically discharged in October 2001. I was months away from the 22-year eligibility point and was not awarded my 'Long Service and Good Conduct Medal'. (LSGC) This deeply saddened me as I came from a police family. Both my father and brother were serving officers and they both received their LSGC's. I felt as though I had nothing to show for my service as a police officer. I was medically discharged due to injuries sustained in the line of duty, through no fault of mine, other than being operational.

The main point I'd like to make on behalf of injured police officers who do not reach the 22-year point (now 20 years), is that recognition, should be clearly part of the medical discharge process for operational officers who put their health on the line in the execution of their duties.'

AUTHOR'S COMMENT

John was a brave officer who was awarded a 'Queen's Commendation for Bravery'.

However, that is not a medal and given his actions I think he was short-changed by not receiving a full 'Queen's Police Medal for Bravery'.

Once again, being only months away from the eligibility period to receive his LS&GC medal, he was robbed of that only by his injury and again in 2010, when the eligibility was reduced to 20 years. John and others still did not receive it because it was not awarded retrospectively.

So, the indisputably brave but medal-unlucky John still has no medal to show even a connection to the police service, let alone to recognise his bravery or health sacrifice.

Having an award in the form of a medal showing that you served as a police officer and were forced to leave through an injury sustained on duty would be valued and is long overdue.

I believe the aforementioned harrowing stories adequately show that more care and recognition for those unfortunately injured and medically discharged from any of the emergency services is urgently needed.

We surely owe them more than they receive now i.e. NOTHING!

We are now ready to move on with Gary's full story.

CHAPTER 4

GARY'S EARLY YEARS

Having now covered a few of the sad stories of other injured officers to highlight the major problem of the lack of care and empathy for those who face danger on a daily basis to keep us all safe, we can now move on with Gary's biography.

Gary Pearson 1977

Gary Pearson was born on 3 June 1953 at Beech Mount Maternity Hospital, Moston, Manchester. His parents were, Harold and Sylvia

Pearson.

Harold and Sylvia

The nurses had his mother marching up and down the ward trying to induce the birth to coincide with Queen Elizabeth II's coronation the day earlier, but Gary failed to show up until the following day. However, he says he still received his commemorative gift of a silver spoon and velvet lined presentation case, given to children born on coronation day.

Gary says that since this initial one-off delayed appearance he has always been early for any appointment but only because he could not stand any further grumbling. Furthermore, he insists that he will not shoulder any blame for not turning up on the 2 June 1953 but instead chooses to somewhat ungraciously put all the blame on his mother.

Gary being the first born, lived with his parents in a 2 up and 2 down rented terraced house in Cromwell Street, Gorton, Manchester. His younger brother, Dean, arrived 3 years later on 17 July 1956. Gary remembers that when his mother brought him home, she laid the tiny bundle on the sofa and even though he was only 3, he says he thought that he had never seen anything quite as ugly but through time he grew to love his new baby brother.

Gary and Dean

Gary's dad, Harold, was a representative with the Manchester Evening Chronicle and his job was to supply newsagents with the current news posters and papers. His wages were sufficient enough to allow his mum, Sylvia, to stay at home. For his work he drove an old Ford Popular motor car with running boards. Gary says he cannot recall the car being used for family days out.

Gary says that as a kid he was left very much to his own devices to seek entertainment. He especially recalls playing on nearby derelict land and using dumped cars to play 'cops n' robbers' little knowing that later in life the games would become only too real for both the brothers.

Living opposite them in Cromwell Street were his great grandmother and his 2 great aunts, Florrie and Olive.

Gary says that there was one strict rule that was never to be broken and that was never to visit his grandmother's house alone. This was because his auntie Olive had mental health problems and had on several occasions threatened to kill him. She was later committed to a hospital for the mentally insane.

The 3 females were the mother and 2 sisters of grandfather, George Pearson, who also lived in Cromwell Street, some 7 doors away. George lived with his wife, Florence and their son, Fred, Gary's uncle and brother to his dad.

GEORGE PEARSON (LATE)

George had served with the Royal Artillery during World War II and was a member of the Desert Rats, a group of British soldiers who helped defeat the Germans in North Africa.

Gary never heard his grandad speak of his war experiences.

The closeness of relatives in the community made family life ideal but unfortunately this was not to last.

Corporal George Pearson

When Gary knew his grandad, George, he worked at Smithfield Market in Manchester city centre, and he frequently brought home a crate of either apples or oranges. He left the open crate unattended on the pavement outside his home for kids to help themselves. This was a rare treat back in the 50s and this made George hugely popular with the neighbours.

Gary's mother's parents, his other grandparents, Ralph and Jessie Leyland, both worked on the railway and Gary and Dean would spend weekends with them in their 2 up and 2 down home in Collyhurst. Gary says they always had Sunday dinner with them.

On New Year's Eve 1958, Gary recalls that his parents along with Uncle Fred, were going out to attend a party to see the New Year in. There was a big row as to which grandparents would look after him and Dean. Thankfully, his mother won, and they stayed with her parents.

The following morning, New Year's Day 1959, Gary's parents arrived at his grandparents' home and broke the sad and shocking news that Grandad George had been killed in a gas explosion at his home. He had died on the way to hospital.

The following article appeared in the newspapers:

'Where three houses collapsed in an explosion and two died. The scene in Cromwell Street, West Gorton, Manchester.

Early on January 1 after an explosion believed caused by gas, three houses in West Gorton collapsed. A man of 59 died on his way to hospital and the body of a widow of 70 was recovered from the ruins of her house. A broken gas main was found nearby.'

It was later revealed that a gas smell coming from a streetlamp outside grandad's home had leaked gas to a pocket beneath 70-year-old widow, Mrs Barrett's home next door. Mrs Barrett was infirm and always slept downstairs in a fire lit room. The gas reached the fire, ignited and blew up causing 3 terraced houses to collapse and killed both Mrs Barrett and Gary's grandad next door.

What an extremely sad ending to war veteran George's life at the age of 59 years, especially when he served in the armed forces during and survived throughout World War II, only to be blown up and killed in peacetime in his own home 13 years later.

FLORENCE PEARSON (LATE)

Gary's grandmother had very few injuries apart from a couple of cracked ribs and they put that down to George shielding her. Fred was not in the house because he was out with Gary's parents at a New Year's Eve party.

Gary recalls that his grandmother, George's widow, consulted a solicitor in regard to the gas board negligence, given that the gas smell was reported the previous day, but nothing came of it. To his knowledge his grandmother received nothing more than being re-housed to a flat.

I believe an opportunity to gain huge compensation was missed. However, it was 1959 and we know our rights a great deal better nowadays.

Florence appeared to the outside world to stoically accept the demolishing of her home and the sad loss of her husband and merely soldier on as usual but in her new flat and without George, by her side.

The transition to electric lighting in the UK was completed by 1968 after the decision was made to stop using gas street lighting following World War II. Factors that contributed to the end include damage from the war, the development of electricity, and competition from electric light sources.

Before gas streetlights were introduced, streets were lit by candles, oil lamps, or rushlights, which were dim and sometimes emitted a lot of smoke. Gas lighting became popular because it was up to 75% cheaper than oil lamps or candles.

Some towns and cities still have working gas lamps and lamp attendants are employed to look after them. For example, London has around 1,300 working gas lamps, with about 270 in Westminster.

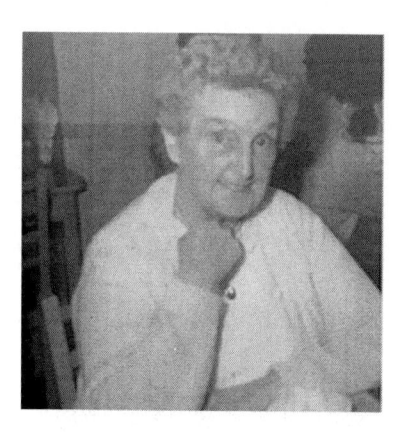

Grandma Florence Pearson

Florence proved to be resilient and although only about 5' 2" she was tough, as many grandmas seemed to be back then. They were the matriarchs and held the family together.

Gary remembers that she would save the newspapers and give them to him to take to the local fish and chip shop where he would hand them over in exchange for a bag of chips. Of course, that all stopped when we all became acutely more aware of hygiene.

He recalls one occasion when he was about 5 years of age, when the rag and bone man was in their street on his rounds with his horse and cart. Grandma Florence gave him a few rags to take to him because Gary wanted a goldfish, which would be given in exchange. However, because maybe the ragman did not have any goldfish that day, he came away with a bow and arrow.

Gary happily played out in the street and fired the arrow. It struck the wheel of a passing bicycle being ridden by a man. The arrow lodged in the front wheel and brought the rider to an abrupt halt, and he crashed heavily to the ground. He was not pleased to say the least and took hold of the young Gary and marched him off to his grandma obviously thinking he would be chastised. Well, he was in for a shock because it was, he who unexpectedly got a slap from the fiercely protective Grandma Florence, saying, "Don't you ever touch him again!" I think that shows the character of Gary's grandma and a lot of the womenfolk back then were the same.

What is also apparent from this story is that Gary was right to swap his bow and arrow to concentrate on his more expert skills with a gun.

Starting with his birth Gary had always had to look after his 3 years younger brother, Dean. From being as young as about 5, Dean had always had a mouth on him and this in the early 1960s in Gorton and Collyhurst, quite rough areas, was a recipe for some kid to strike a blow. Invariably Dean would 'gob off', Gary would intervene, and it would be him who would receive the blow.

Each weekend Gary and Dean would stay at one of their grandparents' homes and this would be alternated. When Gary was about 5 years old, he recalls that the most lucrative weekends for him were always with his mother's parents, Gran and Grandad Leyland.

The boys would be dropped off on a Friday evening and picked up Sunday night. Early every Saturday morning Gary would get up, get dressed before anyone else in the house was up and about and he would be out walking the back entryways of the houses.

If he was lucky, he would find a couple of shillings on a back step and if he was extra lucky, he could find nearly a pound. This would later be spent at a nearby herbalist shop on a drink of cream soda with ice cream on top.

It wasn't until Gary was a little older and was telling his gran about his finds that she shouted, "You silly little bugger, people put money on their back steps to pay the milkman!"

When Gary reached 5 years old, he was able to start school but because the family were living in Gorton, he went to St Mark's Infants School. He says he didn't have a particularly memorable time there and when he was about 6 years old, they moved house to a bungalow on Cheltenham Road in Alkrington. Here he says he thought his dad had won the football pools because they had an inside bathroom with a bath and toilet and a massive back garden in which the 2 boys could kick a ball.

Gary then went to Alkrington Primary School, but he says again nothing of any significance occurred during this period.

When Gary was about 8 or 9 years old, they moved again. This time it was a complete change to what they were used to, in that his parents were managing Clarke's newsagent and sweet shop on Councillor Lane in Cheadle.

Gary says he thought this was great because they lived in the flat over the top of the shop and it always smelled of chocolate, the smell coming from the shop downstairs.

He would often help serve when he came home from school and invariably, he could also be found serving from behind the shop counter at weekends.

Gary says he recalls a woman who came into the shop every day for 6 ounces of Victory V lozenges. These were brown lozenges, and it was his dad who later told him that he thought she could be addicted to them because apparently it was believed they contained some sort of addictive additive.

When Gary told of this, I wondered if there was any basis to the speculation of the addictive properties and I was stunned to discover the following:

Victory V: 'It's got a kick like a mule'.

Victory Vs were not very prepossessing in their appearance, flat, rock-hard brick-like lozenges the colour of dirty khaki. Their decidedly acquired smell and taste was no better: it was more than mildly medicinal and seemed to shoot straight up your nose and into your brain. One might well ask why anyone would want to subject themselves to such an ordeal, and it might have remained a mystery until I discovered the ingredients list. That is interesting in itself since most British food products weren't required to have an 'ingredients list' until quite recently. But Victory Vs originally did have one and I discovered why the product had such a 'devoted band of asbestos-mouthed fans' because two of its active ingredients were, chloroform and ether!

Yes, you read it right: chloroform, the substance in which comic-book villains soak a rag to overpower their victim and ether, the stuff that anaesthetists administer before their patients go under the knife. No wonder so many schoolchildren consumed the nasty-tasting throat lozenges as if they were candy! After you had sucked your way through two or three of those, breathing deep all the while, you were guaranteed to feel no pain.

Victory Vs of today no longer contain chloroform and ether, just simulations of their original flavour, and their sales nowadays have plummeted, most likely due to the public's preference for natural ingredients over synthetic ones. The new slogan is 'Victory V: Forged for Strength'; but it just doesn't have the kick that the old one did.

It would seem that the Victory Vs lozenge manufacturers knew exactly what they were doing and intended to capitalise on the effects of the addictive ingredients.

All addictive substances produce feelings of pleasure. These 'rewarding effects' positively reinforce their use and increase the likelihood of repeated use. The rewarding effects of substances involve activity in the nucleus accumbens, including activation of the brain's dopamine and opioid signalling system.

Now I also know the next mentioned item is also addictive to some. It was in the shop that young Gary first saw a top-shelf glossy magazine. There would be a lot of builders coming into buy the magazines and he always wondered why. He found out when he looked. He says he bets his eyes came out like organ stops. (He assures me that was all that did!) He says he always had a smirk on his face when he served anyone buying these magazines afterwards.

Once again like nomads, the young family were again on the move and this time they moved to Polefield Road. His dad got a job at the nearby brake linings factory and his mother worked in a jewellery shop, again nearby.

Both Dean and Gary went to Victoria Avenue Primary School and again this time it was nothing above the ordinary, except Gary discovering he was a champion. A champion at what you may ask?

At this school, there was an outside boys' toilet which apart from the sit-down cubical the rest including the urinal had no roof. All the boys used to try to pee over the wall on any unsuspecting kids who might be standing on the opposite side of the wall in the playground.

After serious training, Gary managed to hit the dizzy heights, but the only problem was that the girls it hit, screamed and alerted the nearby canteen lady who was supervising the playground at the time, and she discovered what had happened. As everyone in the toilets, apart from Gary, swiftly disappeared with the first scream, he was the only one who got caught. He was taken to the headmistress and that was the end of his playtime for some weeks and forever in respect of his dazzling water fountain display.

On reaching the grand old age of 11 years Gary went to Plant Hill

Comprehensive School where he played rugby for the first time and discovered he loved every minute of it. The school itself was a bit of a rough-and-tumble sort of place with some good teachers and of course some bad.

An incident happened when Gary was in the 3rd year, when he was about 13 and Dean had just started in the first year. During one of the lunch times Dean went to Gary's form room and was clearly in some distress. He said that an older and bigger boy had beaten and kicked him. Dean knew his name, so Gary went looking for him and it didn't take him long. Stupidly Gary didn't have a conversation with the lad but instead grabbed him and punched him in the face. He was told that if he hit Dean again, he'd get much worse.

That afternoon one of the senior teachers went to Gary's class and asked to speak to him. He told him he had seen the boy he'd hit in a distressed state standing in the corridor and had asked him what was wrong. After he had spoken to him, he said it became apparent that Gary had hit the wrong boy. There was mention of severe discipline and possible expulsion from school. However, after Gary said he would go and apologise to the poor boy and that he was genuinely sorry, things calmed down.

One of the subjects Gary enjoyed was geography and he always found it a genuinely interesting subject. However, his teacher mistook his attitude for one of indifference and he was sent to a class of lesser abilities. He soon learned the difference between good and bad teachers. His new geography teacher would enter the classroom, give a page number of a textbook to read, put his feet up on the desk and fall asleep. When he was awake, Gary appeared to be the brunt of his derision, and he would constantly refer to the fact he'd moved down a class.

However, much continued as usual and soon the time arrived to take exams. Gary had already handed in his fieldwork project on places in the

Peak District and now it was time for the exam.

Walking into the gym which was transformed for the exams with single desks and chairs, Gary says on entering he found it quite daunting. However, on settling in he saw the geography teacher look at him and start laughing. Gary says he is not someone who gets easily embarrassed but when you have a full gym of silent students and a teacher openly starts laughing at you, you tend to colour up. He then walked up to Gary's desk and in a voice loud enough for everyone to hear he mockingly said, "Well, Pearson, we all know the one who shouldn't be here, don't we?"

After a couple of weeks, Gary walked into the geography room with his other classmates and he saw all the fieldwork folders on the teacher's desk, they were back from marking. He could see his folder on the bottom, to say he felt sick was an understatement.

He watched as the teacher called out the students' names and each got up in turn to collect their work, and then he finally came to Gary's. He saw him pick up his work and then stare at him. Gary says he decided then if he started ridiculing him again, he was walking out.

Gary saw him stand and holding his folder he walked towards him. Now it was plan B. Gary was bigger than him and because he was now playing rugby every week and was using weights he had bulked up. Gary decided he was going to punch him if he started his ridiculing nonsense again. He says he can still remember all the students staring in his direction and likely expecting fireworks.

The teacher stood in front of Gary's desk and placed his folder on it. He then announced that the Education Authority who marked the fieldwork had sent notice that Gary's fieldwork was flawless and was the first time a piece of work had got 100%. Gary says he thought he was going to be sick and spent the next 40 minutes or so in class just smiling at the teacher.

The icing on the cake came when his original geography teacher invited him to a meeting and apologised. Gary left Plant Hill at the age of 17 years. His mother wanted him to become a draughtsman and had even filled out an application for the position in a factory. Gary didn't want that and so instead he secretly applied to be a Manchester and Salford Police cadet.

Gary's mother was so pleased when her application for him to train as a draughtsman was accepted but not so pleased when he showed her his acceptance to be a police cadet.

Gary says that he was delighted when he won that argument.

He didn't leave school with a mass of certificates. He had his coveted Grade 1 Geography CSE, history GCE, English Language GCE and English Literature GCE. Most of all he just wanted a job.

DEAN PEARSON (LATE)

Dean did not achieve his ambition in that he had from being small expressed a wish to join the Royal Marine Commandos and when he left school, he began asking how he could join. His mother actively worked to stop him from joining and continually suggested he join the police instead saying that when he got to 21 years he could then leave and join the Royal Marines.

Dean did join Greater Manchester Police, but he did not choose to leave at 21. Later he too also became a qualified firearms user, but he never joined the Tactical Aid Group (TAG) and so Gary and Dean never worked together. However, one may say they were true, 'Brothers in Arms'.

Dean Pearson

Gary says he always felt that Dean regretted not joining the Royal Marines.

Gary married his childhood sweetheart in 1977, they had known each other since their schooldays from the age of 13 years. Together they had 2 children, a boy and a girl. His wife is a reserved lady and fiercely protective of her own and her children's privacy. I respect her wish for them not to be included in this book.

CHAPTER 5

GARY'S POLICE STORIES

Gary went to Bruche Police Training College in 1972 for 13 weeks to learn about police procedures to enable him to eventually become a police officer. Whilst there a Merseyside colleague and he devised a plan to have a bit of fun.

The camp commandant would often be seen cycling around the camp on his bicycle and they decided it would be the focus of their prank.

One very early morning about 1 am, they both dressed in black and went out onto the camp, they soon found the bike and took it to the parade ground.

Gary had arranged with some of the policewomen to give them some old brassieres and so he made his way to their block to get them.

Around the female block was a low hedge about 3 feet tall, so he went to push through it but what he didn't know was that barbed wire was either woven through the hedge or had grown around it.

The wire punctured his trousers and hooked into his legs, and this caused him to pitch forward leaving his face on the floor and his legs in the air.

Just at this time the local police did a drive-through to ensure the security of the college.

He heard the giggles of the girls in the block who were in on the lark and were watching the whole thing. Eventually, the police moved away, and he was able to detach himself. He says how they never spotted him is still a mystery.

The next day on parade, instead of the Union flag, there was the commandant's bike and about 8 bras at the top of the flagpole.

By the way, what I did learn from Gary's tale was a bra flown from a flagpole makes a fantastic substitute windsock, but effectiveness much depends on cup size. I am yet to find a reason for the bicycle other than a jolly jape.

The phantom flag hoisters were never apprehended and remain anonymous, but that may change on the publishing of this book.

After finishing his 13-week training at Bruche Police Training Centre, Gary was sent to C Division and stationed at Whitworth Street.

After a chat with an inspector, he was told to go home and come back later, his first shift being nights.

At 10.45 pm that night he paraded and was told by the charge office sergeant that initially he was to accompany a seasoned officer who would show him the ropes.

So it began, he was now on a uniform patrol as a passenger in a signed police vehicle which he thought was great.

After attending a few minor incidents, where he tried to take it all in as to what to do, his training officer declared he'd done enough in the way of tutoring and so the next job they were allocated he wanted to see what Gary could do.

The call soon came, a man was causing an annoyance by walking up and down the road with a 'ghetto blaster' radio.

By this time, it was about 2.30 am and when they arrived at the scene and before Gary saw the man, he could hear this unholy row, just like a hundred cats screeching.

He could see several residents looking out of their bedroom windows, and they were obviously annoyed.

Then he saw him, a Sikh, walking up and down the road, holding a large radio which had the volume on full but not tuned into any one particular station. The noise was deafening.

Gary went to talk to him, but he could not hear him because of the noise, and he refused to turn off the radio and just kept pushing Gary away. So, the decision was made, and he arrested him, and just at this point his training officer appeared and with a smile said, "Tell him you are arresting him for common law breach of the peace."

So that was it, Gary's first prisoner, who he sat with inside the divisional van while he was conveyed to Whitworth Street.

On arrival, Gary told the charge office sergeant why he had arrested the man, his prisoner was processed and his training officer helped him with the paperwork, all the time with a grin on his face.

At 7 am Gary was just ready to go home and looking forward to his bed when his training officer said to him, "Where are you going?" again with the same stupid grin on his face.

He told him he was going home to bed. His grin turned into a laugh and that's when he dropped the bombshell. He told Gary that anyone arrested for common law breach of the peace had to go to the next available court to be bound over and as the arresting officer he had to attend court to give evidence. At 10 am off Gary went to Manchester Magistrates' Court.

So, on his first tour of duty he had arrested his first person and given evidence at court. He arrived home at about 12.30 pm and went straight to bed.

At about 2 pm, Gary was woken up by his mother who was shouting for him to get up while she pulled the bed covers off him. He didn't know what all the fuss was about and just being awoken from a deep sleep he couldn't hear very well what she was shouting.

Eventually, it became clear what she was saying, "Work's been on, that bloody bloke you arrested last night is lousy and I need to wash everything."

Apparently, the lads in the detention centre had found a flea infestation that came from his prisoner. When Gary got up to shower, he found his uniform already in a bucket of Dettol.

He had to relate the story, excuse the pun, from scratch, on many occasions because the smell stayed with that uniform forever, and he was obliged to explain it away.

When Gary first went to his allocated division, the C Division he was told for the first few weeks or so that he would be accompanied by a tutor constable, this however did not always happen.

About 3 weeks into his time at his new division, on turning up for work for an afternoon shift of 3 pm to 11 pm Gary was informed that he was to go to Gorton Section house to relieve the Station Officer (SO) for an hour while he had his refreshments. One of the officers with a police vehicle gave Gary a lift to the Gorton Section house and the SO was able to go for his food.

Whilst Gary had received police training in normal police duties, he had never experienced the running of a satellite police office and so was quite rightly a bit nervous. During the hour he had several enquiries for directions and even had to fend off a man who mistakenly took Gorton Section house as a toilet and was walking in whilst opening his trousers. He was that desperate Gary allowed him to use the police toilet.

After nearly an hour Gary was starting to be less nervous as he was probably realising, he could cope.

At exactly 5.10 pm, 2 young lads, aged about 9 years old, came into the section house and asked him for the time. It was obvious both lads had been to Gorton swimming baths which was just next door, it didn't take Sherlock Holmes to deduce that from their wet hair and towels tucked under their arms. After informing them of the time he heard one say, "Me mam's gonna kill me," then they ran off.

The SO then came back, and Gary went out on foot patrol.

The following day Gary again paraded on for his 3 pm to 11 pm shift but was told he was to go and relieve the SO at Gorton again. He was hoping that this wasn't going to be a regular thing.

On his arrival at Gorton there was no sign of the SO and so Gary went into the back room and asked the two area constables present if they'd seen the SO, weirdly without looking up they just shook their heads to indicate, no.

As Gary walked back to the front desk, he saw a car pull up outside and two suited men got out, they walked into the office and identified themselves as a detective constable and a detective sergeant. They then asked if they were talking to Gary Pearson and Gary confirmed that they were. He was then escorted to what now Gary realised was a police car and was then driven to Mill Street, but during the ride, the detective sergeant (DS) who was sitting in the front passenger seat turned around and said to Gary who was sitting in the back, "Well, you thief, where is it?" Gary thinking this was a joke started laughing, that thought soon stopped when the DS came out with a load of expletives and threats.

On arrival at Mill Street, Gary was escorted to a CID interview room where he stayed without any contact for 2 and a half hours. He had still not been told why he was there, after that period the door opened, and the DS walked in. He asked Gary if he was going to tell him what he'd done with it. Although young in service and really nervous, Gary asked the DS what the hell he was talking about and to explain what he meant by 'it'. The DS started talking about Gary nicking the fiver and where was it?

At last, it was revealed in that the story related to how 2 young lads had found a fiver at the baths and had brought it to Gorton to hand it into the police. They got home and told their mother what had happened, and she asked them for the receipt, but they told her the police hadn't given them one. The mother had then gone to Gorton to get the receipt but no evidence of any fiver being handed in could be found, so she made a complaint of theft by a policeman.

By the end of this, the penny had dropped with Gary, and he explained what had happened and the comment one of the lads had made. He also explained that it sounded like the lads had made the story up because they were in trouble for being late home from the swimming baths. The DS didn't say a word and walked out.

After about an hour and a half the door was opened and Gary was told to step out of the room, as he did, he then saw the SO from Gorton standing in the corridor. It later turned out he was getting the same treatment as Gary. Both the SO and Gary were taken to see the chief superintendent in his office. After they had stood to attention in front of the chief superintendent's desk he immediately went into a lecture on dishonest officers and how there was no room for them in the police, and then he went on to say that it would go on their personal file that they had been accused of theft.

The SO having more time in the job than Gary asked on what evidence they were being accused. Gary had already told the SO what he thought had happened, and so the SO asked if the lads had been re-interviewed. They were told that due to enquiries made by the DS and the DC, they believed that the lads were lying about the fiver as they were late home, they had put this to them in the presence of their mother and they had admitted it.

However, the accusations would show on both their personal files and they were told to get out. Police justice was a bit different from normal justice. Welcome to the police service!

As a young 19-year-old bobby with about 2 months on the job Gary was given a walking beat along Hyde Road, Gorton.

It was late afternoon, maybe 3 or 4 pm, when he got a radio message that there was an incident just up the road. He could see in the distance a traffic holdup and could hear car horns being sounded.

As he got to within about 10 yards of the incident, he could see a medium-sized pony which was obviously agitated. It was kicking out at cars and rearing onto car bonnets with its front hooves.

Now, when Gary was younger, he was an avid reader of the J T Edson cowboy books and in particular he liked a character named the Ysabel Kid who was half Comanche. He'd read that in order to tame wild mustangs he would put his arms around the neck of the horse and bite down firmly on one of its ears.

So, in full police uniform, complete with helmet and maybe due to the exuberance of youth, he launched himself onto the pony and placed it in a headlock. He bit firmly down on its right ear. Well, the poor startled animal went absolutely berserk and threw Gary around like a rag doll. It probably caused more damage and chaos than previously when he wasn't present. It jumped and bucked and crashed into the cars, rearing, kicking and snorting.

Eventually, the pony with him still onboard fell against a bus and he let go. As he sat winded on the floor, an old guy who he hadn't seen before, calmly walked up to the pony and took out a length of string from his pocket, tied it around the pony's neck and led it away.

Somewhat sheepishly, Gary stood up and retrieved his helmet from under a car. He shook the dust from it and trying to look as casual as he could, he walked off into the sunset, whilst spitting out horsehair and to the fanfare of hooting car horns and laughter. With his young ego severely dented and so embarrassed he never told a soul back at the 'nick' or his family.

I think you all will agree that must have been a hilariously funny scene. It's not every day you get to witness on a main street in the UK a scene from a Wild West rodeo, with a uniformed bobby riding a bucking bronco.

It's little wonder that Gary chose to carry on as a copper in preference to becoming a horse whisperer.

Gary may have just answered the long-standing question as to why boxer Mike Tyson savagely bit Evander Hollyfield's ear in their heavyweight title fight in 1997. It has frequently been debated as to why Tyson had behaved so bizarrely.

From Gary's story, I may not be the only one who will now consider a brand-new theory in that Tyson might have also been a fan who read of the Ysabel Kid's unique talent, and he too was merely trying to calm Hollyfield.

One thing I have learned from this tale is if I am ever in Gary's company when he is not wearing a muzzle, I am going to make a concerted effort to stay completely calm, especially when not wearing ear protectors.

Early on in Gary's career he was on duty driving a signed police vehicle around Swinton town centre at about 11 am one morning when he received a radio message to attend at an address on the outskirts of the town.

On arrival, he could see it was a large semi-detached house which was in need of much repair work. A neighbour was standing outside and told him the old lady who lived there on her own had not been seen for about a week and her curtains had remained closed the whole period.

Weighing up what he could do, instead of kicking down the door he went to all the neighbours' houses on the block and eventually got the phone number of her son.

By this time, it was about 1 pm and he was starving hungry. The police station had phoned the son, and he arrived at nearing 2 pm.

Garys says that he was about as much use as a chocolate fireguard and said he hadn't seen his mum for over 2 weeks. No, he didn't have a key to get in, no she didn't have a phone, and no he didn't think it right to kick the door in. What a dipstick!

After checking the downstairs windows, Gary found a rear one to be loose. He could just see through the crack in the curtains what looked to be a body lying on the floor in front of the fireplace. So, with some effort and the dipstick asking him not to damage the window frame he managed to open the window. The smell from the room convinced him he was no longer hungry.

He clambered through the window and entered the dimly lit squalid room, his eyes still adjusting to the lack of light and his nostrils twitching at the putrid smell. He approached the corpse lying on her back and partially covered among scattered rubbish. He bent down beside her and reached out his hand to touch her neck to feel for a pulse.

Suddenly, her eyes sprang open wide, and she yelled, "Get me up!" Well, Gary nearly jumped out of his skin and more, but the end of her sentence was drowned out by his blood-curdling scream.

The poor woman seemed to be shocked too and kept repeating, "Are you alright, are you alright?" After a while with his hand still on his heart, he reassured her that he was but in reality, he was still recovering. It was not supposed to be this reversal of roles.

After sitting her down he radioed for an ambulance because he thought she might have hypothermia. While waiting for the ambulance he explained to the dipstick that he needed to take more care of his mother. In temper he went to the window and slammed it shut, smashing the window.

After the ambulance left, Gary went back to the police station for his meal but with the dodgy smell still in his nostrils he'd lost his appetite.

Gary says that every time he sees a Hammer horror film where either Dracula or a corpse springs up from a coffin that experience comes flooding back to him in an instant.

Come to think of it, Gary, the scene would not have looked out of place in either of the comedy classics, Carry on Screaming or Carry on Constable.

One day in early 1973, Gary was on a morning shift working 7 am to 3 pm and on foot patrol in Gorton. As he walked along the main street, which was filled with shops and people, he saw a vehicle parked up outside a cafe. It was parked on double yellow lines, and it was also causing an obstruction. As he got closer to the vehicle, he could see someone sitting in the front passenger seat of the car and as he reached the car, he could see the occupant was a stunningly beautiful young woman.

On seeing Gary, the woman gave Gary a gorgeous smile and a wave of her hand. So intent was Gary on staring at her he came very close to walking into a lamppost. Just as he was about to speak to the woman a young man came running out of the cafe and explained that the car had broken down, he had gone into the cafe to see if he could use their phone.

Remembering his initial training Gary asked the man what the registration number of the car was but the man explained he had borrowed the car from his mate to take his girlfriend home. Taking out his two-piece police radio, one being a transmitter and the other being a receiver, Gary radioed into the police station to ask the communications officer to check the daily listings of stolen motor vehicles.

There was no police national computer at this time to check car owner's details but each morning the Manchester Criminal Records Office would broadcast details of any reported stolen vehicles. The check came back negative for being stolen. Each time Gary looked at the woman in the car she would smile and give a little wave, he thought she looked like a film star.

After requesting the man show Gary his license and his insurance and being told they were at home, he issued him with a Hort/1, which was a form for him to produce his documents at a police station of his choice.

At this point, the stunning woman got out of the car, and she asked the man if he thought the car would start if she pushed it. Gary opened his mouth without engaging his brain and told them both to get in the car and he would push it. Luckily, the road did have a downward slope, so it wasn't hard to get it going. After a couple of yards, the engine coughed and sputtered into life. The young man stopped the car and winding down his window shouted his thanks, and then drove off.

The following morning when Gary paraded for duty, he was presented by the sergeant with a printed sheet with a yellow line circling a name and car number. Oh no, it was the number of the car he had pushed the day before and..... it was stolen. When Gary later checked the name and address the man had given him it came as little surprise that he found it was all false.

The more Gary thought about it the more he wondered if the car had broken down and if he'd been duped with the woman's presence being an ideal distraction. He wondered too if the pair were still laughing about it.

When you make a mistake such as this in the police it's probably going to be a big one but likely it will help to make it the last one of that particular nature.

By the way, for the benefit of those who are wondering, it was not Bonnie and Clyde because it was not their era and besides it was stated clearly that the car was outside a cafe and not a bank!

It was also in 1973 after Gary had taken part in the police driving examination that having passed the course, he was now able to drive signed police cars, and it was not long before he got his chance to use his newfound skills.

At the duty parade one evening at 11 pm Gary found himself allocated to a mobile beat and the area he'd been given was Gorton, an area he knew well. Driving up Hyde Road towards his beat he received a radio message saying that there was a man lying on the ground in Abbey Hey Lane. It didn't take him long to get to the location and he saw a large group of people standing around a man on the ground.

On getting out of his car he walked to the group and could see the man was bleeding profusely from a deep cut to his left arm. It looked like it could be an arterial wound as the blood appeared to be gushing. Gary immediately applied pressure to the man's wound and knelt on his upper arm attempting to stop the blood, a towel appeared from the crowd, and this was also used to stop the bleeding.

Whilst trying to stop the bleeding a young man approached Gary and stated he was the man's son. He explained that he and his father had gone to a top-floor maisonette directly opposite because they believed the occupant had stolen his young sister's bike. He then went on to say that the occupant had attacked them. With the bleeding under control, Gary asked the son to keep pressure on his father's arm while he radioed for an ambulance.

Gary then walked up the stairs to the maisonette and at the top he could see a large pool of blood and a pane of glass in the front door was smashed. He pushed open the door and found a man of about 20 years' old standing in the hallway. The man was someone Gary already knew, Thomas Jobey. Gary asked him if he'd attacked the 2 men, and he admitted he had but said they had attacked him first. He was then arrested and placed in the police vehicle and whilst in the vehicle Gary asked Jobey what he had used to inflict the wound on the man. He told Gary he had used a garden spade which was in the cupboard in the hallway.

Gary was on his own, so he locked Jobey in the police car and went back to the maisonette to retrieve the spade, but all the time he thought something was not right. When he entered the maisonette, he saw an older man standing in the lounge staring at him. It was only then he noticed the light inside was coming from a single candle. It was not unusual for some homes in the area to have their electricity cut off because of not paying the electric bill.

As Gary walked towards the man, he could see genuine fear on his face, and it wasn't until he looked in the mirror on the chimney breast he saw why. Gary was covered in blood; it was on his face and hands and his trousers were saturated where he had knelt next to the injured man. After calming the man down, it was ascertained that he was Jobey's dad and after Gary asked for the location of the spade, he took possession of it.

As he walked out of the house Gary radioed for the van to attend so he could take Jobey to the police station but as he turned to walk down the stairs he slipped on the blood and fell down 3 or 4 steps dropping the spade and hurting his back. After a quick check, he realised he was okay, so he picked up the spade and went back to the police car, but there was a problem, Jobey had gone. The doors of the police car had been locked from the outside, but Gary had forgotten that they could still be opened by anyone still inside. Such things happen in the 'heat of battle.'

After asking the crowd if anyone had seen where he had gone, they said he had gone back in the direction of his home. So once again Gary went to the maisonette and on entering, he saw Jobey's father and he asked him where his son was, he just pointed upstairs. As Gary was walking up the stairs he suddenly remembered, no electricity and he'd left his torch in the car, the upstairs was pitch black. Each stair seemed to have a creak, and he was trying to regulate his breathing to try to hear something. On getting to the top of the stairs he was presented with 3 doors. So, he decided to turn off his radio and just stand and listen, all the time wondering if he was about to be attacked.

It seemed like hours but probably was only a couple minutes when Gary heard a noise come from the door at the end of the corridor, so he walked to it. Pushing the door slowly open he used his right hand to hold the door but immediately it was slammed shut. It didn't fully shut as Gary's hand was between the door and the door frame, he was sure he heard a crack. Pushing on the door Gary forced his way in, although the room, which turned out to be the bathroom, was in darkness, the window faced the street and so the streetlights did give some illumination.

Gary saw the figure of a man who was holding a razor blade in each hand. Without really thinking and for the first and last time Gary drew his truncheon using his injured hand and hit Jobey on the head dropping him to his knees. By this time the ambulance had arrived and so had the van, so Gary placed Jobey in the van, and he was taken to the police station.

When Gary arrived at the station, he exhibit-bagged the spade and as the assault was a Section 18 wounding it was customary for the CID to take over, but Gary thought something still wasn't right.

By the time Gary had arrived back at the police station his right hand was very badly swollen so he attended the hospital only to have it confirmed that he'd broken 2 bones in the hand. After getting the hand encased in plaster from hand to the middle of his forearm, Gary drove back to the station where he told his sergeant he was reporting sick and he also needed to get out of his blood-stained clothing. The sergeant enquired where Gary lived and then said he only lived about 2 miles from him and as he was thinking of going home early Gary could give him a lift. So, it transpired that the PC who was going off duty injured and with his hand in plaster was driving his uninjured sergeant home.

During the journey home, Gary voiced his concerns about the Jobey case and said it didn't feel right, the sergeant told him that was a CID problem now.

After a period of recuperation, Gary was back at work and the time he had off gave him time to think about the case. How could a garden spade make such a clean cut and not break the arm? How come the majority of the blood was by the front door with the broken glass pane and the blood trail from the door to the street?

When Gary was asked by the CID officer to give him a statement, he asked him if it was possible that the man that was injured could have done it himself by breaking the glass in the front door. He was told the spade had been examined and found to have blood on it and both the injured man and his son were adamant Jobey had attacked them.

Eventually, the day came for the case to go to Crown Court and Gary gave his evidence as he saw it and afterwards, he sat in court to hear the rest of the case. As it progressed it became apparent that there had been an altercation at the front door of Jobey's home and from what was said the man had cut his arm on the glass.

No reason was given as to why Jobey had told Gary he had used a spade, and it wasn't until Gary was walking back to the station it occurred to him that obviously the blood on the spade occurred when he had fallen down the stairs.

Gary had dealt with Jobey before and described him as 'not the brightest button in the box.' An explanation for the involvement of the spade could be that Jobey armed himself with it in self-defence, but it was the broken glass that caused the wound and not the spade. It may also have been that the injured man had broken the glass and that was when his injury occurred.

The mention of the blood on the spade was totally irrelevant because of the amount of blood spilt there was cross-contamination everywhere, especially on Gary who had seized the spade as evidence.

However, justice was likely served when Jobey was found not guilty, and it was probably the right decision.

Gary says that he abhors violence against females and says he has always been vocal about the far too lenient punishments meted out to men who hit women. However, this opinion wavered during the following street incident.

In early 1974, he was driving a signed police car on Hyde Road, Gorton, at about 11.30 pm when he saw a man punching a woman. He immediately stopped and restrained the man who was clearly drunk. He then attacked Gary and he was forced to render him incapable of further violence. As he fell to the floor drunk, he heard this terrible scream and turned around to find the woman had stood up and was screaming that he'd killed her boyfriend.

She then took hold of Gary between the legs in a vice-like grip. He says he'd never felt pain like it, his legs turned to jelly, he had incredible stomach pains and could hardly move. He couldn't even think properly and thought seriously about hitting her but says he just couldn't do that and probably didn't have the strength.

Gary says he doesn't know what possessed him to say such a daft thing, maybe he was influenced by the fact she was squeezing his privates so hard and the sheer ridiculousness of the situation, but he called out, "Ahh, you're crushing me crown jewels!" He felt her grip relax and he was able to step away. Meanwhile, she began to laugh so much that she was sick, and he nearly joined her in his pain. He says that he honestly does not know what made him say it, but he did, and it worked. He says he thought, 'Store that comment away lad it may come in handy again!'

Gary locked them both up for being drunk and disorderly and overlooked the assault on police by the 'Crusher.' Justice was done.

It was certainly an unorthodox way to defuse a heated situation and not in any police textbook but I will bear it in mind for the future.

It was always thought that the best job in the division was the divisional van because it was always double-manned. It was always sent first to any violent disturbances as well as the more mundane divisional jobs, and in early 1974 Gary took his position on the van.

After parading on duty for an afternoon shift of 3 pm to 11 pm, Gary and his partner were driving along Stockport Road when they were flagged down by a man standing in the middle of the road waving his arms. They stopped their vehicle, and the man explained that his daughter had just been discharged from the hospital, but she had collapsed, and he pointed to a young woman lying on the pavement just behind a bus stop.

Both officers got out of their vehicle to render what assistance they could and as Gary knelt at the side of the young girl, it was obvious she was in extreme pain, he saw she was bleeding heavily from underneath her skirt. Not wishing to look closer for any injuries they asked her father if there was any chance that someone had attacked her, but he was adamant no one had. The officers immediately radioed for medical assistance, but they were told it would be about 30 minutes, there were problems with no vehicles being available and traffic was now getting heavy.

The officers could see that the blood loss was heavy, and the young girl seemed to be drifting in and out of unconsciousness and so Gary being the driver made the decision that they would take her to hospital. The young girl lay in the back of the van on their 2 police overcoats and her father was told to hold her tight as the ride may get a bit rough. The old J4 van that Gary was driving was not equipped with 'blues and twos.' So, with headlights on full and hazard warning lights flashing that would have to do.

The ride to Manchester Royal Infirmary was the fastest Gary had driven since his driving course and in all probability scared a few road users, it certainly scared him. Whilst driving, his partner was relaying a commentary to the radio controller who was relating their position to the hospital and eventually they arrived, and the young girl was placed on a wheeled stretcher and she and her father were taken into the hospital.

A quick assessment of the inside of the van showed that it looked like a butcher's shop, it had to be cleaned. The van was driven to Longsight Police Station where the vehicle cleaners worked, and Gary explained to one of the cleaners that the inside of the van needed cleaning. On opening the rear doors, the cleaner just stared at the interior and told them he couldn't clean that, and he would have to speak to a supervisor as it looked like a crime scene. This was getting silly so while Gary hosed the inside of the van, his partner swept it out.

On arrival back at their police station, both officers were met by a sergeant who immediately asked who had given permission to carry an unauthorised civilian in the back of the van and for the van to be driven at speed through built-up areas. Both officers were told at no time were they insured as they could only carry police personnel or persons arrested.

After working with so many long-serving police officers Gary was ready for this and promptly told the sergeant that they had arrested the young girl but had to de-arrest her when they saw she was injured. The sergeant then demanded to know what she was arrested for, to which Gary replied, "She was drunk and refusing to fight, Sarge." The charge office where they were stood with other officers erupted in a fit of laughter, but Gary and his partner remained stoney-faced, even the sergeant had a glimmer of a smile. Both Gary and his partner were told to get back out on patrol.

A couple of days later both Gary and his partner were told that the inspector wanted to see them. They thought the matter had escalated and they were in trouble. On entering the inspector's office, the inspector said, "You pair of lucky sods." The hospital had been on saying they didn't know who the officers were, but they brought a young girl back to the hospital who was haemorrhaging and had she not been brought back quickly enough she would have died.

Gary realised later, that the somewhat mild attempt to administer a telling–off was likely a wind-up, albeit that was never disclosed but even if it was not, then as it turned out it was definitely well worth it.

In April 1974, Manchester and Salford Police amalgamated and became the Greater Manchester Police and the force began to change. One of the changes that seemed to happen overnight was the influx of officers who had previously served in Cheshire and Lancashire and the differences in how people worked, but the one Gary liked best was the influx of new equipment and new cars.

Gary paraded at Whitworth Street at 11 pm one evening to begin his week of night shifts and after the parade, he was told to take his allocated mini patrol car to Longsight garage as it had developed an exhaust problem.

On arrival, he went into the traffic office filled out the paperwork and was given the keys to a replacement vehicle. He was told the registration number and where it was parked.

He entered the car park and found a brand-new police mini. He got into the car and smelled that new car smell. Looking around inside, there was no screwed-up paperwork, no fag ash, no used pens or broken pencils. It was pristine and as he started it up, he immediately noticed that the gearstick had changed, gone was the L-shaped stick that was potluck to find the gear you wanted. Now there was a straight gearstick, which was much more positive.

He radioed in to say he had picked up the replacement vehicle and was driving out to his beat but was told to return to Whitworth Street and pick up a sergeant who had just moved from Cheshire and wanted a tour of the division.

He picked up the sergeant and found him to be a really nice bloke, his name was Ron Astles, and he was keen to see how they worked.

After taking him on a quick tour and going to some jobs, Gary thought he'd show him Gorton Section House (GSH).

To describe GSH as a police station would be rather kind, it was a single-storey brick building that consisted of a small front office which overlooked the main road and Granada Bowl car park. There was a tiny interview room, dining area, kitchen, and outside toilet. All officers assigned to the 'C' Division were allocated a key to gain access.

Normally police vehicles would be parked opposite GSH on the Granada Bowl car park but as he didn't want to get the new vehicle dirty by driving on a cinder car park, he parked it up just around the corner next to Gorton Baths and they walked the 25 yards to GSH. As the building was only open from 9 am to 5 or 6 pm and it was now about 2 am it was locked and so using his key in they went.

He showed the sergeant around the building and as they were about to leave the front office the phone rang.

Gary picked the phone up and identified himself and the voice on the other end explained that he was the manager of Granada Bowl, and he had just seen two males attacking a police vehicle parked near Gorton Baths and they were now walking towards GSH.

Gary dropped the phone and ran outside, closely followed by the sergeant and he saw two lads walking towards them. They grabbed them and took them back to where he'd parked the vehicle. As they turned the corner, horror of horrors, the brand-new beautiful police car was tipped on its side. It had been on duty for only 3 hours.

Gary says that he cannot really describe his feelings; he supposes the sudden death of both these yobs would probably not have been enough. While he was still standing looking at the extensively damaged vehicle and trying to form some intelligible speech a car drove up. The passenger window was opened and the driver leaned out and asked if everything was okay. Gary was fuming and glaring at the driver and just blurted out, "Does it bloody well look okay? Go on, on your way." At that, the driver wished the officers good night and drove off.

Gary looked at Sergeant Astles and indicating to the inquisitive driver he said, "Bloody idiot!" The sergeant with a big grin on his face then said, "He's quite a nice bloke actually. He was my superintendent when I was in Cheshire."

In 1974/75 Gary and his partner PC Alan Wright worked on a van together and paraded for a night shift of 11 pm to 7 am. Working on the van was one of the duties Gary really enjoyed, and it was usually good fun working with a colleague but sometimes it did have its dark side. The van was usually first at any potential disorder and this particular evening was no exception.

At about midnight, whilst out on patrol, they received a call to attend a domestic dispute between a husband and wife. When they arrived at the address, they could see the door was open and the front downstairs window was smashed. They announced their presence, went in and sat on a chair in the kitchen was a young woman about 30 years old, she was very upset and looked dishevelled.

The officers asked her if she was okay and what had happened. The woman was reluctant to say anything at first but slowly she said that her estranged husband had come around, he was drunk and wanted sex. She had refused to open the door, so he'd smashed the window and kicked it open, he'd then come in and raped her. She told the officers that she was glad her daughter, aged about 12 years old, had not come downstairs to see anything, but went on to say she was probably used to it as this wasn't the first time it had occurred.

The officers asked her if she needed any hospital treatment, but she declined. She thanked them but refused to take the matter any further. Gary was feeling a bit out of his depth but tried to persuade her to make a complaint, but she was adamant she wouldn't. She was asked how many times this had happened, and she replied, "Whenever he gets drunk." When asked where he lived, she said that she had no idea.

The officers attended at this address on two further occasions, the calls of a disturbance coming from neighbours but each time the woman wouldn't support any further police action.

On the last visit Gary made to see her he gave her his name and work telephone number.

Some 4 weeks later Gary was crewed with Alan again and he received a radio message to attend at the woman's home, she had asked for him by name. On arrival it was a duplicate of previous visits, the front door had been kicked in. When Gary entered the house, he found the woman just standing in the front room staring. He asked if she was alright and what had happened. The woman said he'd kicked the door in again but this time he didn't want her; he wanted her daughter, and she couldn't allow that. Gary asked her what she meant, and she pointed to the kitchen.

When Gary went into the kitchen, he saw that a chair had been knocked over and he could see a pair of legs sticking out from alongside a kitchen table. Gary went to the body and checked for a pulse but couldn't find one. At the side of the body was a large kitchen knife, it was covered in blood and the blade was badly bent.

Gary went back into the front room; he noted that the woman looked calmer, and he asked her what happened. The woman said again that he had wanted her daughter and tried to push her aside to get to her, so she stabbed him. The daughter was with a neighbour because the woman knew what was going to happen when the police arrived.

The deceased had been stabbed 5 times in the chest and once in the back. It is believed that the back wound was the one that proved to be fatal.

Gary radioed for an ambulance and the CID to attend. While Alan stayed at the scene, Gary took the woman to the police station. On the journey to the station, Gary told the woman to ask for a solicitor. He also told her to give his and Alan's details to the solicitor because they could give evidence as to her previous attacks.

Both Alan and Gary gave statements of not only the arrest but also the full circumstances leading up to it.

Gary was later told the prosecution had dropped the charge against the woman at the Crown Court. The reason for not proceeding is thought to have been because the lawful excuse of 'self-defence' was accepted.

Although at the time they had UK residency both the woman and the deceased had Polish origins.

Gary said there were two instances whilst he was working that really got to him. The first one has just been detailed and the second time was also in the 1970's.

Gary was on foot patrol around the streets in Gorton, it was a Sunday at about 6 pm and he was looking forward to something to eat as his shift had started at 3 pm.

As usual, he could see women talking to neighbours, their husbands were probably in the local pub having a pint and kids were still out playing football when he saw at the other end of the street a group of about five women obviously in deep conversations.

As soon as they saw Gary, they began waving for him to go to them. He'd not been in the job long and was hoping whatever they wanted he could deal with it. As with all groups there is inevitably a spokesman. It was explained to him that in the house they were outside of, lived a young woman of questionable virtue and she had two small children.

The concern was that since Saturday they had heard the children crying and one had been seen banging on the upstairs front window, but the mother had not been seen. Gary says that he hadn't a clue what to do but he went and knocked on the door but didn't get an answer. One of the women shouted that the child was back looking out of the upstairs window.

He could see the child, but it was too young to speak to him or even open the front door. So, making the decision, he radioed in and asked to see a sergeant for advice, but the section inspector said he was close by and would attend.

On the arrival of the inspector, Gary outlined what he knew but admitted he didn't know what to do. Wrong move, the inspector immediately asked what he thought should be done and to justify the decision with what lawful powers there were to take those actions.

Gary could see the group of women staring at him and listening intently to their conversation. Gary said, "In my opinion, two children are possibly in danger and their mother could be incapacitated and unable to answer the door, so I should put the door in."

Gary could hear the women agreeing and surprisingly so did the inspector. So, a size ten boot met the front door, the door lost, and entry was gained.

The place was a tip, there were empty beer and wine bottles all over the floor, dirty clothes and the smell was appalling. After a quick check of the downstairs, Gary went upstairs and opened the front bedroom door where he had seen the child. He says he'd never seen anything as bad, before or after.

The bedroom floor was full of used dirty disposable nappies, and the smell of urine and human waste was so bad he could hardly breathe. On the left-hand side of the room was a cot and it contained a small child, probably no older than twelve months. The child was filthy as was his bedding. Gary saw the child standing holding onto the cot for support and could see just how thin it was.

When he looked around the room, he saw another child and guessed it to be maybe two or three. The child was also filthy and was wearing just a vest, it was so thin he could see its bones. What was strange both children didn't make a sound, they just stared. Then the child in the cot held out its arms to be picked up, so Gary did and hugged it. He came very close to tears.

As was the system at this time, policewomen had their own department and were only just starting to be incorporated into mainline police duties. The policewomen dealt with females and children and so two women colleagues came and took over.

He couldn't stop thinking about these children and after about a week he went to ask what had happened. He was told that their mother had gone with a male friend to Blackpool on the Friday evening leaving the children with a loaf of bread and jam if they got hungry.

The police thought it serious enough to go ahead with criminal proceedings against the mother and to involve social services with a view to get the children into care and possibly into fostering.

How can a mother treat her children like that? Disgraceful!

Gary suggests that all police officers have at least one case which brings back vivid memories. He says that he has a few that affected him and even now nearly 50 years later he still finds them upsetting.

One such case occurred in the late 1970s, when he was on duty driving a police vehicle on Hyde Road, Gorton, at about 11.30 pm, just after the pubs had kicked out. He received a radio call saying that someone had been assaulted.

He had an idea that it was in all probability a couple of drunks and so he drove to the address. As he walked to the front door, he could see that the house was in darkness, so he wondered if it was a false call, but he banged on the door anyway.

A couple of seconds later, he heard a woman's voice asking who it was. He identified himself and she opened the door and asked him to come in. Although the woman looked upset, she didn't look as though she was hurt.

As they walked down the hallway, he asked her what the problem was. She explained it wasn't her but her friend who had been attacked by her partner.

The walked into the main lounge and he could see a young female lying face down on the floor with a towel over her. The young girl was conscious but couldn't speak because she was sobbing hysterically.

He knelt down by her side, and she screamed, "Don't touch me. Don't touch me!"

Gary asked her friend to tell him what had happened, and it was explained that she and the young girl had been out but had gotten home later than expected and her partner who was very jealous had attacked her.

He told her that he needed to see where, if anywhere, she was injured so he could assess what action to take.

Her friend knelt down beside the young girl and asked her if it was okay to show Gary and the answer must have been 'yes', and she lifted the towel away.

The whole of the girl's back was a mass of bloody stripes and on some, he thought he could see bone. He immediately summoned an ambulance and while waiting for its arrival he ascertained that the girl's partner had whipped her with a telephone wire and then had left.

After he had obtained the partner's name and description and the ambulance had taken the girl to hospital, he spent the next couple of hours driving around the area. If ever there was a man Gary wished to meet it was the young girl's partner.

Gary then received a radio message from the station to say the girl's friend had phoned because she had just seen the partner return home.

He got to the address and banged on the door and on answering it, and seeing a uniformed bobby, our hero completely caved in, crying and saying he loved the girl, and he didn't mean it. Gary says he has never wanted someone to attack him as much as he wanted this low life to attack him but unfortunately, it was not to be, and he took him to the police station to charge him with the wounding.

Over the next couple of weeks, he took witness statements from the friend and young girl who had been so savagely attacked. He explained that she would have to give evidence at Crown Court but had nothing to fear and just to tell the truth.

The day for court came and unusually it was early morning at Minshull Street Crown Court. As Gary sat outside the courtroom waiting for the witnesses, he looked down the corridor and to his utter astonishment, he saw the young girl walking towards him holding hands with her attacker partner. She told Gary they were back together, and she wouldn't be giving evidence against him.

Gary looked at the CID officer who was also on the case and he walked off. Why would anyone allow another person to inflict such violence upon them and not want justice?

The case was withdrawn.

As a police officer you must learn to get used to frustratingly radical changes of mind when partners are involved in such cases.

However, time has moved on and nowadays this instance of extreme violence would likely proceed with the aggrieved party being forced to give evidence and treated as a 'hostile witness' if a plea of 'not guilty' was entered by the defendant.

In late 1976 Gary was in the plain clothes department and wore as the name shows normal civilian clothing. They were used to check on licence premises in the division and also parts where crime was high and any uniformed officers' presence would prohibit catching the perpetrators because they would be easily spotted.

One evening as Gary went back to the office, one of the officers from the charge office was sitting waiting for him. He told Gary his brother Dean had contacted the station to speak to him and it was urgent. Not knowing where Dean was, Gary rang home, and Dean answered the phone. He explained to Gary that their mother had been attacked and was being treated in hospital. Gary immediately left work and drove to Crumpsall hospital.

On entering A&E, Gary found his mother sitting in an examination room, her white blouse was covered in blood, and she looked dreadful. She explained that she had parked her car and was walking home when someone grabbed her and pulled her into a back entry at the rear of the shops. The coward held his hand over her mouth and then with his other hand produced a Stanley knife and slashed her chest, whilst doing so he said, "Tell Gary, remember black Friday!"

I don't think anyone who has never experienced anything like this could possibly know what thoughts Gary had at this time. It took several days for the rage to diminish and sensible thoughts to return. His mother had not seen her attacker and he had disguised his voice. When he ran off, he pushed her to the ground, so she didn't even see him run away.

When Gary spoke to the CID officer in charge, he admitted they had nothing at all to go on.

Gary got out his pocketbooks for the previous 2 years and went through every Friday he had worked to see if anything stood out, nothing did. Whilst he was checking his pocketbooks a colleague came into the office. He had heard about the assault and said how sorry he was. He told Gary he had an informant who knew everything that happened in the area where his mother was attacked and did Gary want to meet him. That was a big 'YES'. Strangely the colleague told Gary they would have to wait until 3 am or 4 am.

At 3 am the journey started with his colleague driving to an area in Manchester known as Cheetham Hill. The car was parked at the front of a row of large double-fronted terraced houses. Following his colleague down a path to the front door of a house his colleague knocked on the door and as the door opened a gust of hot air hit them along with something else, the overwhelming smell of cannabis.

They walked down the hallway to the main room at the rear of the house and on entering Gary realised he was in a shebeen. Shebeens are unlicensed drinking houses, the majority set up by people from the West Indies, where they can meet up to play cards or dominoes, drink and of course openly smoke cannabis with little fear of detection and prosecution.

The colleague asked Gary to wait where he was while he went to speak to his informant and after a couple of minutes, his colleague waved Gary to join them. What followed was Gary explaining what had happened to his mother and his desire to meet her attacker, but Gary got the distinct impression the informant knew nothing. With a promise to let them know if he heard anything the informant left.

His colleague told Gary that they made a great goat curry and suggested they have one before going back to the police station. Being a bit hungry and never having tried goat curry, Gary agreed and very soon 2 steaming plates of curry were put in front of them. The curry was great, probably one of the best he had tasted if not a little heavy on the chillies. After consuming the meal, they then went back to the station and got on with their jobs.

In 1977 Gary now found himself in the Tactical Aid Group (TAG) and he loved working with such a great group of men. At first, they were used to prevent serious disorder and stop violence at football matches as well as raids on pubs and clubs but later their duties were extended.

One evening they were told they were to go on a raid, but the location was being withheld until they got there. Equipped with a universal door opener, a 16lb sledgehammer, Gary with the others boarded the TAG van.

On arrival at the scene of the operation, all the officers got out of the van and Gary saw immediately it was the shebeen he had previously been in and where he had been served the goat curry. The officers were instructed to enter the building and so the 'universal door opener' was produced and entry was swiftly gained.

Inside there were approximately 30 to 40 men and none of them presented any threat but by the time there had been a cursory search of the whole property, there was a great pile of cannabis wraps discarded on the floor. The process then began by taking names addresses and samples of the drinks. Gary was having a search in the rear of the property and was checking the kitchen area. He could see a large pan of goat curry on low heat on the stove, so he turned it off.

Looking in a large cupboard at the side of the stove Gary found approximately 8 or 9 boxes and when he opened them, he found each box to contain 12 tins of dog meat, but the place didn't have a dog but the waste bin at the side contained several empty dog food tins.

It became crystal clear that it wasn't goat curry, it was dog meat curry and being heavily laced with chilli it covered any taste that maybe would have been a sure giveaway clue.

Gary says when he saw the dog food tins, the memory of the 'goat curry' he'd eaten there came flooding back to him and he was very nearly sick. Since then, he has tried to convince himself that the one he'd been served was genuine. Erm! I'm not so sure but what do you think?

The shebeen was swiftly closed down and has long since been demolished with shops taking the place where it stood but there will still be many people who will remember the best 'goat curry' they've ever had, not knowing the truth.

No one was ever arrested for the shocking assault on Gary's innocent mother. Gary does not wish to comment any further on that because his understandable anger still remains to this day but as he says, he cannot do anything about it except try to put it to the back of his mind.

Perhaps it was a blessing in disguise that the informant was unable to provide Gary with the name of his mother's cowardly attacker. Nevertheless, it was a dreadful shame that the offender was never brought to justice for such a heinous crime and against an innocent female in her sixties.

Unsurprisingly, Gary now avoids goat curries, in the same way as he does strawberries. You will read shortly, why the strawberries!

All of the Greater Manchester Police (GMP) Tactical Aid Group (TAG) members were trained to be firearms officers, this enabled GMP to have a large number of officers trained in firearms should the need arise, and Gary was a member of TAG for a period.

During 1977, an incident occurred during his service with the TAG, and it brings a smile to Gary's face when he thinks of it. He and other officers had been called to a suspicious bag left in the doorway of the South African travel company in Manchester city centre. They formed a cordon around the area to stop people walking near it and the bomb squad had been contacted.

It appeared though that an inspector was not interested in waiting, he walked up to Gary and said to his horror, "Let's go take a look." As they walked towards the doorway all Gary could think of was, 'Yea tho I walk through the valley of death.'

They were about 25 feet from the bag when the device went off.

Luckily, the device was very small and although it did damage the travel company doorway thankfully the inspector and Gary both escaped being injured. However, it did nothing for the inspector's nerves because he was ashen and trembling. Back at the police station he was told to go home.

It wasn't long before news filtered back that the inspector had gotten into his car to drive home and had reversed it into the chief superintendent's vehicle causing considerable damage.

I guess it just was not the inspector's day OR was it? What do you think?

During October 1977, whilst Gary was in the TAG, they were used to flood an area with police officers to carry-out house to house enquiries after a murder had occurred.

Manchester was currently rocked by a particularly gruesome murder that was attributed to the Yorkshire Ripper. His Manchester victim Jean Jordan known as Scottish Jean was murdered in Moss Side near Southern Cemetery.

Gary was given the area used as allotments by the local community to grow their fruit and vegetables. He had interviewed several allotment owners this particular day but as is often the case with such routine enquiries he had not received any useful information, when he came upon an old chap with the biggest vegetables he'd ever seen.

He got chatting to him and he was more than willing to show him what he'd grown in between answering his questions regarding the murder. He made a brew on his Primus stove, and he offered Gary 3 of the biggest strawberries he'd ever seen. On tasting them, he found them to be very sweet and juicy, just like strawberries should taste.

Eventually, he had to go but before he went, Gary asked him how he managed to grow such large vegetables and delicious fruit. He winked, tapped his nose and beckoned Gary to follow him.

They walked behind his old shed and he could see what looked like a pile of newspapers. Gary said, "That's it?" The old guy just smiled and said, "Yes, but I poo on a sheet of paper and cover it with another sheet and keep doing it until I have a decent pile, then it rots down, and I put it on my fruit and vegetable."

Gary says he managed to get about 50 yards away before he threw up. You may not be surprised to hear that since that experience, whenever Gary is offered strawberries, without disclosing why, he asks, "Is there any other choice on offer?" He says, 'So, you are very welcome to my portion of strawberries and....... cream!'

During Gary's time with TAG, he was involved in the armed escorting of many high-profile Category A prisoners including, the Yorkshire Ripper and the Black Panther.

A Category A prisoner is a prisoner who is considered to be a high risk to the public, police, or national security if they were to escape. They are held in high security prisons and are subject to the most restrictive security measures. Here are some examples of offences that may lead to a prisoner being considered for Category A:

Attempted murder, manslaughter, wounding with intent, rape, indecent assault, robbery or conspiracy to rob, firearms offences, importing or supplying Class A controlled drugs, possessing or supplying explosives, offences connected with terrorism.

Category A prisoners are held in prisons with advanced surveillance systems, scanning systems, and a high staff-to-inmate ratio. The goal of these prisons is to prevent escapes and maintain control over potentially violent or disruptive prisoners.

They house male prisoners who, if they were to escape, pose the most threat to the public, the police or national security.

A prisoner's categorisation can change over time based on their current risk, behaviour in custody, and efforts towards rehabilitation.

Peter William Sutcliffe (2 June 1946 – 13 November 2020), also known as Peter Coonan, was a UK serial killer who was convicted of murdering thirteen women and attempting to murder seven others between 1975 and 1980. Two of Sutcliffe's murders took place in Manchester; all the others were in West Yorkshire.

He was dubbed in press reports as the Yorkshire Ripper, an allusion to the Victorian serial killer Jack the Ripper. He was sentenced to twenty concurrent sentences of life imprisonment, which were converted to a whole life order in 2010. He died on November 13, 2020.

Donald Neilson (born Donald Nappey; 1 August 1936 – 18 December 2011), also known as the Black Panther, was an armed robber, kidnapper and murderer. From 1971, he committed a series of robberies of sub-post offices; in 1974, he killed three men during these robberies. In 1975, he kidnapped Lesley Whittle, an heiress from Highley, Shropshire, who died while in captivity. He was arrested later that year, convicted of four counts of murder, and sentenced to life imprisonment in July 1976. Neilson remained in prison until he died in 2011.

In 1978 after being involved in crowd control at a football match at Old Trafford football ground, the home of Manchester United FC, Gary and his TAG colleagues were on a mobile patrol around Manchester city centre to ensure that there was no disruption caused by any football supporters.

As usual, there were no real problems and so at about 11.30 pm they were stood down to return to the station and as their shift ended, they got into their respective cars and drove home. There were several colleagues who lived in the Wigan area, and they always shared a car for transport to and from work.

On this particular night as they were driving home, they saw a man walking near the motorway and so they stopped their vehicle to ascertain what he was doing. Without going into too much detail whereby the man might be identified, the conversation that took place will be skipped over. However, there was a controlled drug substance found on the man and a conversation ensued between him and the 3 TAG officers, the culmination being that the man disclosed information regarding a large number of drugs.

The following day when the officers returned to work a full meeting of the TAG took place, the theme being that the officers had been told that drugs were being manufactured in a terraced house on Canal Row in Wigan. As they were unaware of this location Gary and 3 other officers were sent to do a reconnaissance of the area.

To say there was no cover was an understatement, the area consisted of about 8 terraced houses in what can only be described as a field, you could literally see for miles around and anyone trying to do observations on any of the properties could be seen immediately. It was decided that one of them would walk down the street and Gary drew the short straw, so trying his best to look nonchalant Gary walked down the street towards the fields at the end.

It wasn't hard to pick out the house they should be focusing on; all the curtains being closed and even from outside you could smell the cannabis being smoked.

After a brief conversation, the officers decided on a long-range observation and that's what took place. Over a couple of days, lots of men and women were seen coming in and out of the building and a decision was made to get a search warrant for the premises.

The raid on the premises took place at about 4 am and the front door was swiftly smashed open, the idea being to enter the premises while the occupants were still wondering what was happening. When the TAG officers entered the premises, they were met with a sight not easily forgotten.

The officers need not have rushed because on the floor in the front room were some 8 men and women, all appeared partially clothed, but they were clearly 'out of it.' There was drug paraphernalia all over the place and also what looked to be a large amount of cannabis resin but what the officers found unusual was the number of jars containing mushrooms, they even found mushrooms in the oven.

All the occupants of the house were arrested for being suspected of being in possession of a controlled substance and were conveyed to Wigan Police Station. When anyone is arrested on suspicion of being in possession of drugs, the suspected drug substance has to be forensically tested by an expert to ensure that is a genuine controlled drug.

The 4 TAG officers started the labour-intensive job of exhibit-bagging and labelling every piece of equipment and suspect substance they discovered. They also took the mushrooms including those in the oven.

Eventually, the premises were thoroughly searched, and every item was exhibit-bagged, and everything was taken to Wigan Police Station and entered in the evidence log.

Some weeks later the officers got the news from the laboratory that they had certainly found cannabis resin, but the big surprise was that the mushrooms were in fact Psilocybin mushrooms or magic mushrooms and were a class A drug, and they had been prepared by drying in the oven. This was the first arrest for the Psilocybin mushrooms in the Greater Manchester area.

Gary and his 3 colleagues received a Chief Constable's Commendation for their dedication to duty.

Psilocybin is a psychedelic compound found in over 200 species of fungi, including magic mushrooms.

Psilocybin is a naturally occurring prodrug that is biologically inactive until converted to psilocin by the body. Psilocin is a serotonergic psychedelic that produces mind-altering effects.

Psilocybin can cause euphoria, visual and mental hallucinations, changes in perception, a distorted sense of time, and perceived spiritual experiences. It can also cause adverse reactions such as nausea and panic attacks.

Psilocybin is found in many species of fungi, including members of the genus Psilocybe, Panaeolus, Inocybe, Pluteus, Gymnopilus, and Pholiotina. Some of the most potent species are P. azurescens, P. semilanceata, and P. cyanescens.

Psilocybin is also known as 4-phosphoryloxy-N, N-dimethyltryptamine (4-PO-DMT). It was previously sold under the brand name Indocybin.

WOOLWORTH'S FIRE

As a general rule, there was always a TAG presence in Manchester city centre mainly to arrest offenders who stole out of delivery vans while the driver was taking goods into the store.

It was 8th May 1979, around lunch time, Gary and a colleague were driving around the city trying to spot potential offenders. As they drove towards the centre of Manchester a call came over the main control room radio that a fire had been reported at the Woolworths store. As they were only a short distance from it, they decided to attend.

They were close when they got the call so were one of the first responders. On arrival, they found smoke coming from the building and a chaotic scene. They could see people running out of the store through the main entrance and milling about outside.

They immediately tried to clear a passage for people to get out of the store but being dressed in scruffy civilian clothes people were ignoring them. The smoke was billowing out of the second-floor windows and people could be heard screaming.

Gary knew there was a fire exit at the side of the store, so he and his colleague ran around to open it. The door was securely closed but they tried to push it with the vehicle, but the angle of the wall stopped direct contact with the door. He could hear people screaming behind the door but just couldn't get it open and all the windows appeared barred so they couldn't gain access through those either. Gary says that he has never felt so useless.

Very soon the Fire Brigade lads arrived so they stepped back. Gary saw those brave firefighters risking their lives trying to gain access to the store but from where he stood it looked like all the windows had bars on them.

As more tenders arrived, Gary and his colleague were just in the way and as they were in civilian clothes with a plain van, they would have looked like two nosey blokes, so they left it to the professionals.

The fire rages inside Woolworths' store.

Gary still thinks about those poor people who were behind that door. Perhaps it could have been a mother with her child or grandparents with their grandchildren and as time has gone on the thoughts haven't dimmed.

What happened?

At around 13:30 hrs. on Tuesday 8 May 1979, a radio operator from a taxi firm called 999 to say that one of their drivers had seen smoke coming out of the Woolworths' store opposite Piccadilly Gardens in the centre of Manchester. Her call was followed by 11 others and fire crews were dispatched to the store.

Crews arrived to find smoke billowing from the six-storey building and people calling for help from the windows. It is thought there were around 500 customers and staff inside the store at the time. Firefighters fought for two-and-a-half hours to bring the fire under control, helping people out of the building via doors, windows and the roof.

At 15:51 hrs., officers declared that the fire was surrounded, and a thorough search of the building was carried out. By that point, 10 people had lost their lives, 47 were taken to hospital for treatment and six fire officers had been injured.

Why was the fire so deadly?

The fire was, at the time, the city's worst fire disaster since World War II and the fire service identified three reasons why it was so deadly.

The first was that it started after a damaged electrical cable ignited furniture made of polyurethane foam, which produced large amounts of thick toxic smoke. The smoke not only caused breathing problems but also obscured the exit signs. The investigation into the fire found most of those that died were in the restaurant on the second floor, but the smoke was so thick, they could not find their way to the exits.

The second reason was that the store had no sprinkler system, which meant it was not until fire crews arrived that any real effort could be made to extinguish the flames.

The final reason was that the upper windows of the store had thick iron bars on them. Fire crews made attempts to pry the bars off the windows with axes and crowbars but were unsuccessful and had to wait for specialist cutting machinery to arrive. As a result, there was a delay in allowing the windows to be used as a means of escape.

What was the legacy?

After the investigation into the cause of the fire found the foam used to fill the budget furniture was to blame for the smoke, Fire Officer Bob Graham decided something had to be done to ensure that such a tragedy could not happen again. He had led the investigation and after it, he joined with other campaigners to persuade the government to change the law and oblige furniture makers to use flame-resistant foam.

In 1988, The Furniture and Furnishings (Fire) (Safety) Regulations, external came into effect, forcing manufacturers to make furniture fillings and covers from safer materials.

It is little wonder that this horrific and sad incident stays with Gary. It highlights the type of shocking experience all emergency service personnel have to deal with and the after-effects on their mental health.

Whilst in the TAG all members were trained in the use of firearms. This enabled GMP to have a large number of qualified firearms officers available should they be needed.

Gary joined GMP TAG in 1977 and he became a qualified firearms user of most weapons issued by GMP, but he specialised in the .38 Smith & Wesson revolver and pump action six shot shotgun, his choice of weapon being the latter. He adopted a nickname for his own Marlin 6 shot pump action shotgun and that was Esmeralda, taken from the name of Quasimodo, The Hunchback of Notre Dame's, female friend.

TAG members usually wore uniform, but the firearms users did not except for a bullet proof vest. Gary normally was dressed in casual shirt, jeans, Barbour wax jacket and boots.

On 14th October 1979, two divers from a local dive club were diving in a flooded quarry near Chorley, Lancashire when they came across a body weighted down with bricks. When the body was recovered it was found that the hands and teeth had been removed to try and thwart any chance of identification.

Days into the investigation two women attended at a police station and told police that the body was that of Martin Johnstone. They also told police that the murder was connected to Terry Clark. Both women were taken into protective custody and several TAG officers were initially used as their protection detail.

When Clark was arrested, he was remanded in custody and taken to Strangeways Prison in Manchester. As Clark was classed high risk it was necessary to have armed police covering the prison.

Gary and 9 colleagues were given this task, and they covered the prison each night. As they could not enter the prison with firearms it was necessary for them to remain outside but still cover all entrances and exits.

They didn't really understand why they were guarding the prison until the third or fourth night when a colleague from the Serious Crime Squad happened to be driving past Strangeways and saw their van.

He stopped and had a chat giving the story about Clark. When Gary pushed him as to why they were there he explained that Clark had allegedly tried to bribe a police officer, and he had also told the arresting officers he'd put the word out he would pay millions to whoever could help him escape.

He went on to say if someone was going to get him out it could possibly be with the use of fully automatic weapons and probably a helicopter.

It put a whole new perspective on what we thought to be a routine protection job.

Convicted offender:

Terrance John Clark (12 November 1944 – 12 August 1983), also known by the aliases Terry Sinclair, Alexander James Sinclair, Tony Bennetti, the Australian Jackal and Mr Big, was the head of the Mr Asia drug syndicate, which imported heroin into New Zealand, Australia and the United Kingdom in the 1970s. Clark was the 'second' head man of the syndicate and became the lead having successfully plotted the murder of Marty Johnstone, the man who became known as Mr Asia.

Clark was ruthless as controller of his operations and killed several associates including Gregory Ollard, a Mr Asia drug supplier and heroin addict. He lured Ollard to Ku-ring-gai Chase National Park in the northern suburbs of Sydney, where he killed, mutilated and buried him. After killing him, he drove to the home of Ollard's girlfriend in Avalon and abducted her. He then drove her to the Blue Mountains where he killed her.

Brief details of the case:

In October 1979, Clark had Marty Johnstone (Mr Asia) lured to Britain on the pretext of a drug deal to take place in Scotland. Johnstone was murdered by his longtime friend Andy Maher under the orders of Clark, and his handless body was dumped in Eccleston Delph, Lancashire, mutilated in a hasty but failed attempt to foil identification by the police.

Maher not only cut off his hands but battered Johnstone's face hoping to prevent dental identification. Initially, the police were unable to identify the victim and published a death mask of Johnstone in several newspapers to assist in identification. In the end, Johnstone was identified by his neck medallion that was still on the corpse. Only one of Johnstone's hands was recovered by police.

Clark was convicted of the contract murder and sentenced to life imprisonment. His trial at the time was the most heavily guarded in British history. He died in 1983 at HM Prison Parkhurst on the Isle of Wight. The official cause of death given was a heart attack.

POPE JOHN PAUL II

In 1982 whilst on secondment in the firearms department Gary was told he was to be a protection officer to Pope John Paul II on his visit to the UK.

Pope John Paul II

Gary is not the one with the cloak, he's the one on the extreme left with dark hair.

Gary was told he had to wear a blue suit, which he didn't have and couldn't afford and so his mother-in-law stepped up to the plate and helped him out. Gary's brother-in-law was currently serving in the Navy but had left his suit at home. After shortening the trousers as his brother-in-law was taller than him, he was then in business.

Come the big day when the Pope came to Heaton Park, Gary found himself at the base of the stage. After His Holiness gave mass, he came down among the selected people in the fenced enclosure and stood at the side of Gary, who could see all the cameras focused on the Pope and he knew he'd also be in shot.

It was at this point a very elderly and over-excited nun launched herself at the Pope. Gary caught her in mid-air, and she struggled like mad to try to touch him, but he restrained her, all the time trying not to hurt her. As he looked around a group of nuns came and took their sister away and he realised everyone was staring at him. When Gary looked at the Pope, he thought he had a smile on his face and later on a member of his entourage told him it had amused him.

Gary later found out his mother had videotaped the whole episode off the TV and every Christmas after that it was played to the amusement of the whole family. He still has the video tape.

I suggest that Gary must have been extremely well regarded to be chosen to be part of the protection team because as a VIP they do not come any higher than the Pope.

Gary was very experienced by then and had seemingly learned two valuable lessons from his earlier experience when he tried unsuccessfully to restrain the startled pony in a headlock. Firstly, to choose a lesser wrestling opponent in the nun and secondly, thank goodness, he had also dispensed with his, as learned from the Ysabel Kid, ear-biting calming technique.

Additionally, one must note that not to be outdone by His Holiness, Gary with his altered suit, also became a 'man of the cloth.'

Pope John Paul II's visit to Manchester on May 31, 1982, was the first time a reigning pope had visited the United Kingdom. The Pope celebrated Mass in Heaton Park, where an outdoor altar was built for the occasion. More than 250,000 people attended the Mass.

However, what Pope John Paul II and Gary did have in common, was both miraculously survived having been shot.

The Pope was shot in 1981 and Gary 1983, one year either side of their meeting in 1982.

On 13 May 1981, in St. Peter's Square in Vatican City, Pope John Paul II was shot and wounded by Mehmet Ali Ağca while he was entering the square. The Pope was struck twice and suffered severe blood loss. Ağca was apprehended immediately and later sentenced to life in prison by an Italian court.

The Pope forgave Ağca for the assassination attempt. He was pardoned by Italian President Carlo Azeglio Ciampi at the Pope's request and was deported to Turkey in June 2000, where he was imprisoned for the 1979 murder of left-wing journalist Abdi

Ipekci and two bank raids carried out in the 1970s.

Ağca converted to Roman Catholicism in 2007. He was released from prison on 18 January 2010, after almost 29 years behind bars.

In 1983, a year after he had been a protection officer to the Pope, Gary was back in uniform on the F Division waiting to return to firearms for another term. At the time in GMP it was deemed important that officers did not stay in specialised departments for extended periods.

One afternoon, Gary was driving a signed police vehicle around Swinton centre, it was about 4 pm, during the summer so it was warm and shirt sleeve order had been authorised. As he drove behind the main shopping centre a man driving his car towards him began flashing his lights. He stopped and he ran over to my vehicle where he explained that he had just been in the car park, and he'd seen a man in a red mini acting really strangely.

Gary thanked him and drove into the car park to have a look around. It was not unusual for teams of shoplifters to use an old car to come to shopping centres, steal goods then return to the car and drive home. Gary thought the suspicious man might be a gang's driver. It didn't take long for him to find the car and he saw someone sitting in the driver's seat.

Gary drove around to the rear of the vehicle and he could see the occupant seemed to be looking through the windscreen at the road below. Gary got out of his vehicle and walked towards the driver's door, and he saw that the window was open.

As he got to the side of the car, he bent down to speak to the occupant who must have sensed Gary was there because he looked up at him. Gary was stunned to see he was wearing a mask. He immediately looked at the front passenger seat where he also saw a double-barrelled sawn-off shotgun. In a split-second Gary says Mr Fear and Mr Adrenaline kicked in and he says he doesn't even remember opening the driver's door and dragging him out, but he did.

He radioed for a van to take the suspect to the police station. As they waited for the vehicle the man was quite talkative and told Gary he intended to rob the pub which he had been watching. He said he knew the landlord had not banked the takings from the night before.

Gary safely secured the weapon, found it to be unloaded and a check showed that the car had been stolen earlier.

When Gary got back to the station, he found his prisoner had been whisked away to the CID office, which he didn't mind as he was not a fan of paperwork. He was told it wasn't the man's first attempt at committing an armed robbery.

Gary says a 'Well done, lad' would have been appreciated but nothing that even came close to a word of praise was ever mentioned.

Gary's courageous and quick-thinking actions deserved more than a 'Well done, lad' and at the very least deserved a Chief Constable's Commendation. My experience is that for every one awarded many more brave acts are sadly overlooked.

I'm not a chief constable and it is 40 years too late, but I believe I can speak for all in saying, 'Bloody well done, lad!'

On 5th November 1983, Gary had been back in firearms for several weeks, when the call came for him to attend at a Manchester Serious Crime Squad office.

They were briefed that there was reliable information that a jeweller was to be attacked at his home, and he would be robbed of his cash and stock. They were told the attackers would be armed. The problem with this job was that the jeweller and his wife were elderly, and they had a daughter with special needs.

It was decided that Gary and 3 others, who were to be armed, would stay in the house, while another team would be hidden nearby. It was arranged that a covert spotter would give updates as to what was happening outside. It was also realised that they needed to keep the couple out of the area should firearms be used and so a policewoman was brought in to keep the family upstairs. Gary and the 3 others went into the house, closed all the curtains and put the lights on, and the couple and their daughter were taken upstairs. They were listening to constant updates on vehicles passing and any pedestrians. After about 2 hours the same vehicle was seen passing several times.

As Gary and the other 3 all moved closer to the door, the covert spotter said the vehicle had stopped and 2 males had got out and they were carrying a bag. The spotter gave constant updates on what they were doing. Eventually, the 2 males stood in the covered entrance where they had taken a sawn-off shotgun from the bag.

By this time, they could be heard talking outside about how they were going to hit whoever opened the door, force their way in, tie everyone up and force the jeweller to say where his cash and stock were.

Just at that time, the daughter of the couple came down the stairs and it was quickly realised action had to be taken and swiftly. It was decided to leave the house by the side door and confront the two would-be robbers in the front garden.

To the shouts of, 'Armed police, standstill!' they were confronted by 4 shotguns pointing at them and they were quickly disarmed and handcuffed.

They were conveyed to the police station where the Serious Crime detectives charged them with various offences.

This particular incident has stuck with Gary because normally after such a job the perpetrators are whisked off, charged and he would hear no more.

On this occasion it was different because in early 1984 several of the TAG's were told to attend Crown Court to give evidence because the offenders had entered pleas of 'not guilty.' This meant that they would have the opportunity to say exactly what happened. They were convicted and received a prison sentence.

Gary gave evidence wearing an eye patch. The reason being that although he was not to know it at the time but after being involved in successfully disarming and arresting the 2 offenders without anyone being hurt, he would be shot during a firearms training exercise precisely 10 days later.

Gary says he doesn't think Greater Manchester Police was particularly liberal with giving praise or Chief Constable's Commendations to its officers for their hard work, but he did manage to get two.

His first commendation came in 1976 when he was serving in the 'C' Division. During the first six months of 1976, he arrested 27 persons, 14 of whom were for crime, one of those arrested was the woman for killing her husband with the kitchen knife.

His second commendation came for the 'drugs bust' while he was serving in the TAG, when they had carried out extensive covert observations on a group of terraced houses in the Wigan area as it was suspected that the occupants were involved in the sale and supply of drugs.

Subsequently, four houses were raided, and nine persons were arrested, and a quantity of drugs were recovered. Several of those arrested received prison sentences, while others received conditional discharges.

Although not a commendation, he also received a report of appreciation from the Regional Crime Squad Co-ordinator for his part in the attempted armed robbery at the jeweller's home.

Gary certainly deserved more recognition for his brave acts than he ever received. However, this is not unusual being that bosses are often too preoccupied with their own self-promotion than their own officers' courageous actions which are far too frequently overlooked.

As when they were kids, throughout their lives Dean continued to draw his protective elder brother into situations that were not necessarily of Gary's choosing. Nothing much changed as time went on in this respect as another example will show in regard to an incident that happened many years later in adulthood and after Gary had been shot.

In the mid-1980s, Dean invited him to join him for a day at the races. It will be noted, both Gary and Dean were in the police then, but Gary had by then lost his eye. The duo duly met up with a load of other police officers all on their day off, boarded a coach and were taken to the races. A great day was had with loads of beer consumed and Gary won nearly £200 but alas Dean didn't pick one winner. It was soon time for them to get back to the coach and so they started to walk out.

At the exit was a man playing the bagpipes in full Scottish kit. Now Dean had a thing about the tune 'Flower of Scotland' played on the bagpipes. After relieving Gary of £10 he went to the piper and asked him to play the tune and dropped the £10 into the box in front of him. With the requested tune drifting over them, Dean appeared to be in heaven.

However, it was to be spoiled by 3 drunken yobs who came shouting along the path. They stopped in front of the piper and attempted to highland dance. Becoming bored with that they then tried to lift the piper's kilt bringing the tune to a halt as the piper tried to stop them.

This galvanised Dean and Gary says that he knew what was coming. Dean walked over to the yobs and asked them to, 'Please, stop' as he was listening and enjoying the rendition. Gary had a strong feeling of what might be about to kick off, so he took up a position at the side of Dean. The yobs started to call Dean names suggesting he liked men in skirts, and then, oh dear, one of them pushed Dean. The yobs hit the floor very quickly and probably their inebriation helped but they didn't look like they were getting up anytime soon. Gary's hand had swollen up and he thought he'd broken it, but they really needed to get back to the coach and so they left pretty swiftly.

Needless to say, they missed the coach and had to get a train back to Manchester, Gary paying of course but they laughed nearly all the way home, especially when one of them recalled the Scottish saying of 'Up yer kilt!'

'Up yer kilt' is Scottish slang and a toast or dedication like 'cheers' or 'down the hatch'.

The word 'kilt' comes from the ancient Norse word kjilt, which means 'pleated.' A kilt is a knee-length garment that wraps around the body, with pleats at the back and sides. Kilts are traditionally tartan patterned and made of twill-woven worsted wool.

Kilts are a symbol of Scottish heritage and patriotism and are often worn to special events. They are also associated with strength and bravery, due to their roots in Highland warfare and the British Army.

CHAPTER 6

GARY IS RUSHED TO HOSPITAL

The sequence of events has been kept in chronological order as far as possible and we have now reached the stage immediately after Gary had been shot.

Gary's account of the shooting has been briefly related at the start of this book and will be covered in more detail later in his witness statement and 'cold case' review. So, there is no need to repeat it again here. We can go straight to what took place after the shooting incident.

Gary was rushed to Carlisle hospital. He cannot remember much; his face had swollen so much he could not even see through his right eye and the pain he was feeling was intense.

Eventually, he heard someone come into the room where he was lying and tell him they were going to give him something for the pain. He felt someone take hold of his arm and then he felt a needle being stuck into him.

He has a memory of waking up in a darkened room with a small light shining over his head. He could hear voices but soon drifted back into unconsciousness.

The next thing he remembers is intense pain in his face and head and initially, when he opened his right eye, he didn't know where he was. A nurse must have seen him waking up and went to him and helped him sit up, she offered him some water and pills for the pain.

He could see he was in a ward full of men wearing sunglasses and says they looked like Roy Orbison wannabes. He later found out they'd had cataract operations.

Then everything came back to him, he touched his face and felt the dressing over his left eye. He asked the nurse what had happened to him, and she said he'd had an operation to his face and the doctor would discuss it with him.

He drifted in and out of sleep but then he heard a voice he knew; it was his wife telling his son to find Daddy.

When he opened his eye, he watched his wife walking past the bottom of his bed and saw her look at him and walk on.

Calling to her he saw her turn around and stare at him and from the look on her face he could see that she hadn't recognised him. His wife and son walked back to his bed and his son on seeing him burst into tears because Gary supposes to a two-year-old he must have looked pretty scary. A nurse came over and apologised and put a pair of sunglasses on him which hid some of the damage.

His wife explained that the Scottish police welfare had arranged for her and their son to stay at a nearby boarding house so she could be nearby until he was discharged from hospital.

On his first day in the hospital, he was in a lot of pain and really didn't know exactly what the damage to his face was. He had asked the nurses, but they just said the doctor would tell him. That didn't really fill him with confidence. That evening, he was asked to go to the ward office and speak to the doctor. Apart from a very low desk light, the room was in darkness. He could see a machine that tests eyes on the desk and the doctor told him to sit down.

He explained that he had significant damage to the left side of his face, and it was also probable that his left eye had been damaged beyond repair. As the swelling was reducing, he wished to examine the eye more closely and he directed him to place his face on the machine so it might be examined.

After five minutes or so he was asked to sit back and could see from the doctor's face that the news would not be good. The doctor explained that the eye was so badly damaged it would have to be removed. He told him the optic nerve had been severed and if the eye wasn't removed it could affect the sight in his right eye. He also said that if he agreed he would also try and remove some of the foreign matter in his face and head but the largest piece he would have to leave in. He showed him an X-ray of his head and he could clearly see lots of fragments in his cheek and head, but the largest piece looked to be lodged at the back of his left orbit.

The doctor then asked him what he thought the object was that had caused the damage to his face and why was it not magnet-attracting. The penny dropped then, the largest piece of material was round and about a centimetre across and looked just like a primer from the bottom of a cartridge. Could it be from a blank? He told the doctor he had no idea what it was but agreed to the operation for the eye to be removed. He asked the doctor when the operation would be, and he was told that he would personally do it and it would be in the morning.

Gary was in a bit of a panic now and he explained that there was a Clint Eastwood cowboy film on TV the following night and asked if he would be able to see it? The doctor looked at him as if he was daft and just shook his head and said, "I don't think so."

He had a really terrible night's sleep, the pain in his face was horrendous and he had a banging headache, but morning came, and he was wheeled down to the theatre and soon oblivious to everything.

When he woke up, he was back in the ward, and it seemed the pain wasn't as bad. He managed to get up and sit at the table in the ward for lunch. He then slept on and off but at eight o'clock that evening he was up and sat in the TV lounge watching the film.

One of his secrets, that only a handful of people know about is that whilst he was in hospital, his friends brought him two bottles of whisky.

During one evening, he was going to watch the TV. He'd hoped for an action film, but he was just going to check to see what was on and decided he'd take a small glass of whisky with him while he watched.

As he poured the drink out, one of the guys in the ward shouted across that he'd like a drink too and it ended up with Gary pouring everyone in the ward a small dram.

Gary doesn't think he'd been watching TV for more than ten minutes when a nurse came into the room. She looked really annoyed and asked if it was responsible to be giving his fellow patients whisky. He said he thought it was and did she want one.

He then had to sit through a lecture on alcohol affecting the stitches on a person who had just had a cataract operation. Needless to say, he missed the film, and the whisky was poured down the drain.

THE GUINEA PIG CLUB

I include this next piece in regard to the Guinea Pig Club only to show what medical professionals' attitudes were in the past when dealing with the mental effect of those who suffered severe facial disfigurement.

If Gary received his injuries from the 1940s onwards, he may have been transferred for treatment at the famous Queen Victoria Hospital East Grinstead, West Sussex, which specialised in facial reconstruction along with other specialist procedures.

If Gary had been a patient there he would not have been forced to pour away the whisky and you will soon learn that a more relaxed approach was taken to such considered trivial matters, whilst focusing on the more important matter of rehabilitation and boosting the mental state of those so horrendously maimed and disfigured.

I currently live in Hastings, East Sussex some 40 miles from the hospital.

About 30 years ago I sustained a serious injury to my arm, and I was transferred to the Canadian Wing (Ward) of the hospital.

It was as an enjoyable experience as any residency in a hospital could be in that the atmosphere was totally relaxed. As you will read, the 'wing' as the ward was called was still maintained at Canadian expense in gratitude for the treatment their injured airmen received during the war years.

Patients had bottles of spirits and beer on open display on their bedside lockers and were allowed to visit the Guinea Pig pub if not detrimental to their treatment. All this was based on a tradition left over from the war years and you will learn why by reading on. I did not witness any abuse of any of the privileges or relaxed ambience whilst I was a patient at the hospital.

The Guinea Pig Club, established in 1941, was a social club and mutual support network for British and Allied aircrew injured during World War II. Its membership was made up of patients of Archibald McIndoe in Ward III at Queen Victoria Hospital, who had undergone experimental reconstructive plastic surgery, including facial reconstruction, generally after receiving burns injuries in aircraft. The club remained active after the end of the war, and its annual reunion meetings continued until 2007.

The club was established informally in June 1941 with 39 patients, primarily as a drinking club, and rapidly won McIndoe's endorsement.

In 1943, a dedicated Canadian wing was built at the hospital, on the initiative of the Royal Canadian Air Force and at Canadian expense.

At East Grinstead, McIndoe and his colleagues, including Albert Ross Tilley, developed and improved many techniques for treating and reconstructing burns victims. They had to deal with very severe injuries: one man, Air Gunner Les Wilkins, lost his face and hands and McIndoe recreated his fingers by making incisions between his knuckles.

Aware that many patients would have to stay in hospital for several years and undergo many reconstructive operations, McIndoe set out to make their lives relaxed and socially productive. He gave much thought to the reintegration of patients into life after treatment, an aspect of care that had previously been neglected. They were encouraged to lead as normal a life as possible, including being permitted to wear their own clothes or service uniforms instead of 'convalescent blues', and to leave the hospital at will.

There were even barrels of pale ale in the wards – partly in the interests of re-hydrating patients whose injuries had left them dangerously dehydrated, but also to encourage an informal and happy atmosphere.

Local families were encouraged to welcome them as guests, and other residents to treat them without distinction: East Grinstead became 'the town that didn't stare'. The Guinea Pig Club was part of these efforts to make life in the hospital easier and to rebuild patients psychologically in preparation for life outside.

One of the pubs in East Grinstead, frequented by patients, adopted the name 'The Guinea Pig'. Their attendance at the pub was positively encouraged by McIndoe because he wanted his patients to get used to being back amongst the public again. The pub closed in 2008 and was demolished in 2009 to make way for a social housing development named Guinea Pig Place.

The club had not been disbanded at the end of the war and continued to meet for over sixty years. 2007 marked the last reunion. It attracted over 60 attendees, but in view of the survivors' age and frailty the decision was then taken to wind the club down.

However, Gary was not in East Grinstead but instead the Carlisle hospital. He had been there for three days when he was told the consultant was coming to speak to him. The doctor examined his face and discussed the options. It was explained that he had sustained a considerable loss of tissue and bone to the left side of his face and would need skin grafts and an orbital rebuild. He explained that all this would have to take place back in Manchester as the injury would have to stabilise before anyone could operate.

Gary could see he wanted to say more but he appeared to be holding back but eventually, he said, "You do realise that you cannot continue as a police officer with only one eye?"

He thinks then it probably hit him, before he had only pain and blinding headaches to think about but now he felt sick that the doctor was right in that he couldn't continue as a police officer.

When the doctor had gone it took a while to process what he had said, and Gary decided to look in a mirror at his injury. He had not looked before as he probably didn't want to see how much damage had been done.

He hadn't washed for a couple of days because he had been in bed. He asked a nurse if he could have a shower, and it was agreed he could, but a student nurse would have to accompany him as he was unsteady on his feet.

Gary says it was the weirdest feeling, stripping off while being observed by a pretty nurse who then began spraying him with a shower while he cleaned dried blood from his face and hair.

After he had washed and dried himself, he felt able to take his first look at his face. It was still swollen and badly bruised but the wound in his cheek looked horrendous and for the first time he realised just how badly he had been injured.

When his wife came to visit him, they discussed the prospect of Gary having no job and the problems of paying the mortgage and bills, it was just as if his world had ended.

It wasn't until he returned home and was invited to the office Christmas party that he learned that although he was never going to be allowed out operationally again, he was to be given a job in an office.

After about five days in the hospital, Gary had a visit from the doctor who explained that the wound on his face had settled and that was it as far as the treatment they could give at this stage.

He explained that he would need further surgery in order to correct the missing tissue and bone but that would mean either staying in Carlisle or returning home and visiting his own doctor.

So, it was arranged that the police would send a car to collect Gary and his family and take them home. Thankfully, the driver who was sent was his very good friend Alan Rhodes, someone he had served with whilst in TAG.

The journey itself although uneventful was his first experience of being out of hospital. Gary says that every bump in the road they went over felt like someone was rattling his skull and it felt as if his one remaining brain cell was rattling around.

By the time they arrived home, he had a blinding headache and the pain in his face was intense. He had not been given any painkillers, so he had to rely on only paracetamol, which luckily but only partially did the trick.

For the next couple of months, Gary was left to sort himself out. Not once did he receive a phone call from any senior officer in the police. Any contact with the force welfare officer was that it appeared they didn't want anything to do with him and certainly did nothing to help.

He initially went to speak to his own doctor primarily to seek something to stop the pain. He told of suffering strange mood swings and had developed a loss of short-term memory. He also explained that he was having trouble sleeping and when he did, he would suffer nightmares of being shot over and over again.

At the time there was no thought of post-traumatic stress disorder (PTSD) and so he was merely told he'd had a traumatic injury and the feelings would pass. His doctor, however, did refer him to the eye hospital in Manchester and after a short period he received a letter to attend a clinic.

His first visit was to the chap who made prosthetic eyes. He made a temporary eye that could be used until he'd had the surgery to address the cheek tissue and bone issues.

On his first and last visit to the eye examination clinic, the doctor he saw was sitting in a darkened room, except for the light coming from the eye examination equipment.

What Gary says he found incredibly embarrassing was that all the people being seen were sitting and waiting their turn in a line in the room where the examinations took place. When Gary's turn came, he was sat down and was first asked to give the history of his injury.

An eye examination for cataracts or eye defects is not invasive or particularly embarrassing or upsetting. However, Gary's was because he was asked to remove his false eye and in front of perhaps ten people, which understandably was not something he was happy about. Without going into detail by explaining exactly what he said to the doctor suffice it to say that Gary left and never returned.

Gary told his wife he wouldn't be going again to the eye hospital clinic, but he did wonder if his outburst at the hospital had something to do with his feelings being all over the place. He supposes in retrospect that he was suffering from depression, but he didn't recognise it at the time.

He did contact his doctor as he wished for an appointment to discuss further pain control and if he could go somewhere else for treatment.

Gary engaged in deep discussion with his wife about money problems and what they could work out to prioritise payments for mortgage payments, food, gas and electricity. He says he believes his depression and constant pain made all his worries seem considerably worse, albeit they were in a dire financial situation.

As they say, 'Every cloud has a silver lining' or does it, really?

His wife had studied their bank account including every payment coming in and out. There was one payment going out to the TSB bank but oddly she didn't know what it was for.

A phone call to the TSB at Blackley was made as Gary was with that bank before they were married but after, their main account was moved to Santander, his wife's bank, and with whom the mortgage was obtained before marriage.

After jumping through hoops to prove who he was the bank explained the payments were to BUPA. The penny dropped! He had joined BUPA on a cheap plan for police and didn't want to cancel when he was married. So, he arranged to keep his old TSB account open and made a standing order with Santander to send money to the TSB to continue the payment to BUPA and then forgot all about it.

WOW! Gary then knew he had private medical insurance. Was this the much wished for saviour silver lining, as far as the best available private medical treatment was concerned anyway?

After the revelation that he was still in BUPA he rang them the next morning. He explained what had happened and that he undoubtedly needed corrective facial surgery. It was confirmed that Gary was fully covered and there was just no problem and thus the sick with worry feeling he'd had disappeared. He says he then realised that he would no longer have to put up with the cattle market of the NHS and obviously felt total relief.

Within a couple of days, he received a phone call from the secretary of Mr Clive Orton and this surgeon would turn out to be a lifesaver.

When he first met Mr Orton, he related what had happened. He was sent for X-rays and scans and then options were discussed. Within a week or so Gary was in a private hospital, and it was like a whirlwind of actions. He says he didn't really have time to think about what was about to happen.

It was surreal, one minute he was waiting to go into surgery and the next minute he was waking up in his room. He could feel pain in his face and when he reached up to touch his cheek he could feel a dressing. The realisation hit him, and he knew he'd been in surgery, and it was then that he was excited to see the results.

Mr Orton came to see him to explain what he had done to correct the damage to his face. He had rebuilt the cheek using titanium plates and had removed tissue from the inside of his mouth to build up the lost tissue in the orbit of the eye. He also had to stitch the eyelid together for the orbit to heal level. He explained that as the left side of the face had dropped, he had made an incision from the left ear to the side of his head to lift the face and then stitched it in place.

Gary confesses that right then he wondered if he'd look like Frankenstein's monster.

He was in hospital for two days then he was allowed to go home but thankfully this time he had some very strong painkillers.

He had to visit the hospital several times to have the dressings changed and to have the eyelid re-stitched after the stitches had broken because his eyelid tried to blink.

As his face healed, he had several more corrective procedures but only to make the face more symmetrical. He was always awake, and he describes it, as unsurprisingly, not a pleasant experience.

Gary's face was now beginning to heal, and he was told the dressings could be taken off. He says he really couldn't believe what a great job Mr Orton had done. His face was level, his cheek although scarred was not sunken and a lot of the damage had been repaired.

After a couple of weeks, he decided that he would like to get back to normal. So rather than continually wearing a pad over his left eye, he had a black leather patch made and used black elastic to secure the patch.

To give his wife, him and the new eye patch an airing, Gary took them out for a curry and afterwards called into a local pub, which he describes as a big mistake. He has no idea why but each time he went to the bar to get drinks he weirdly had various young ladies approach him and start a conversation. When he got home, he could see his wife was agitated and he soon found out why. He was told the patch had to go and he would have to get a prosthetic eye.

NOTE. Once the story relating to this black leather eye patch and the attraction to young ladies reached the author, Tom Curry, he too has somewhat strangely taken to wearing a similar eye patch when out and about!

Gary contacted BUPA and enquired about the possibility of them covering him so he could get a prosthetic eye, and they agreed. He made an appointment with Mr Robin Brammer who he had previously met at the eye hospital and had been told that he held private surgeries to make patients prosthetic eyes.

At a meeting with Mr Brammer, he discussed all about the procedure and he also explained that prosthetics were not made of glass but a material similar to plastic but here is a more detailed description:

'Modern glass eyes are made from cryolite glass, a specialized white glass that is biocompatible and translucent at high temperatures. The coloured parts of the eye, such as the iris, pupil, and veins, are made of coloured glass that is melted onto the cryolite.

However, most prosthetic eyes today are made from acrylic plastic, also known as PMMA (polymethyl methacrylate). Acrylic is more resistant to bacteria than glass and can last longer.

A prosthetic eye, also known as an ocular prosthesis, is a shell-shaped device that fits over an orbital implant and under the eyelids. It replaces a natural eye that has been removed due to an enucleation, evisceration, or orbital exenteration. An ocular prosthesis does not provide vision, but it can be made to look natural with painted irises and pupils.'

Gary had to attend several sessions where he saw his prosthetic eye take shape, including how the eye was painted, and he thought it was incredibly authentic. Eventually, he was fitted with the prosthesis and although the effect was not perfect it wasn't bad either.

During Gary's last visit to Mr Brammer, he mentioned that a surgeon who is based in America was visiting England, to operate on a young girl who had lost an eye, and he had developed a pioneering procedure.

It was explained that he used a piece of sterilised coral which was put into the orbit of the eye and eventually, the flesh would grow around the coral which would then move and in turn, allow the prosthetic eye some movement. A peg could also be attached to the coral and then attached to the prosthetic eye giving it even more movement.

Coral implants are made of porous material, meaning tissues can grow into the implant. Examples are hydroxy-apatite (coral-like), polyethylene (Medpor) and Aluminium oxide (Alumina). A recent development is coated implants such as Bioeye, where the implant has a soft coating to which the muscles can be attached.

Gary agreed to have the suggested procedure done but it turned out to be the most painful he was to ever experience. However, as the orbit healed for the first time, he felt the prosthetic eye move. Needless to say, he did not have the peg fitted.

Gary says if he'd been given the option of which eye to lose, he'd have chosen for it to be his left, as it was, because his right eye was his dominant. He found this out when he first fired a gun, and the following is an easy test to find out which is your dominant eye.

Keep both eyes open and focused on a distant object, say a mantle clock or similar, then extend your arm out and point with your index finger or thumb at the object. Alternately close one eye at a time. The eye that keeps your finger directly in front of the object while the other eye is closed is your dominant eye.

Gary has never used a firearm since his injury, but he did teach his children the dangers of guns and how to use an air rifle to show them how to shoot, much to the disappointment of stallholders at the fair in Portsmouth when his daughter shot for prizes.

He thinks the only thing that still really affects him quite badly is sudden bangs. He says that if his grandchildren have balloons and one suddenly bursts, he could nearly be sick.

PETE RAMSDEN

A quote from a retired fellow GMP officer:

'In 1979 I was a detective with the GMP force Drug Squad. As such, I was trained and qualified as an Authorised Firearms Officer (AFO), and I was thus qualified to carry a weapon when operationally necessary in the execution of my duties. Being an AFO requires regular and varied training to maintain the high standards demanded for the role.

Towards the end of 1983, having lots of contact with Firearms Officers, I heard about the serious incident involving Gary Pearson. Whilst details were initially sketchy, I heard that a Foreign National, undergoing firearms' training had tampered with a weapon, during his training.

The story went that although the weapon was loaded with blanks, something else had been inserted into the chamber and when he discharged it, this resulted in a life-threatening injury to Gary. People were angry at the unbelievable stupidity of the action that had taken place.

Sometime, not much later, I was up at the GMP firearms range at Diggle in the Pennines on a refresher course and there was probably about half a dozen of us training. The incident was still fresh in my mind and although I didn't know Gary personally, everyone was horrified about the incident and wanted to know how he was doing, so I asked our instructor.

I never forgot the story that followed. Although tragic, it still makes me laugh to this day and I have recited it on many occasions. It says so much about Gary's character. It is so typical of the people I worked with and encapsulates what I loved about being in 'The Job'. It still makes me proud.

We were told that Gary had been discharged from hospital and when he was due to leave, one of his close mates went to collect him.

So, Gary got in the car, and there was just the two of them. Normally, we are told, they would be chatting away and there would be banter, but understandably on this occasion there was nothing said. We were told that there was a really, really, uncomfortable and prolonged silence as they set off driving.

The injury was so devastating, the future so uncertain and gloomy that Gary's mate, who was driving, just didn't know what to say under the sad circumstances to break the awkward silence. This carried on agonisingly for about 5 minutes until they stopped at a set of traffic lights. Then Gary nonchalantly said, "I spy, with my one and only eye, something beginning with..." At that the ice was broken, and a resemblance of normality resumed.

Many outside the job won't appreciate the black humour but it got us all through so much adversity.'

AUTHOR'S COMMENT

Gary says he has no recollection of this, but he was heavily sedated even when discharged from the hospital. However, he did add that it does sound like something he would say.

If Gary did say it, then it is typical of his fantastic humour and upbeat character.

What is certain is that Gary was always determined not to be seen as a victim. He had always thought that people who believe they are victims are not in a good state of mind. He didn't hate anyone and thought being bitter would not only ruin his life but that of his family members too.

CHAPTER 7

GARY RETURNS TO DUTY

Gary returned to work at the police station in March 1984, but it was made plain from the outset that his role was behind a desk. He could never go out operationally again.

After being shot, Gary admits he got a little sick of people telling him he would no longer be able to do something or other. The biggest cause of annoyance was people saying, "You'll never be able to ride a motorcycle again." So, he set his stall out to do just that.

As he was now office-bound and working at the police station in the centre of Manchester, he knew he could park the bike in the yard and save paying for car parking. He had to buy a new bike as 12 months previously he had given his brother his 650cc Yamaha. Getting a bike was easier than he thought, and he also acquired a brand-new white police crash helmet, a bright yellow, fluorescent jacket and over trousers. He says he looked like a banana on drugs!

So it began, helmet, fluorescent jacket and trousers on, he started his rides to work. He says he believes he looked so bright you could possibly see him from space.

Things went great until one morning when he had ridden about a mile from home a car suddenly pulled out of a side road on his right, not his blind-side. Now if the car had just kept driving it would have been okay, but he didn't, he stopped directly in front of Gary. He remembers seeing the startled face of the driver looking straight at him just as he smashed right into the side of his car. Gary went right over the top of the vehicle banging his head on the roof and hitting the road about 10 feet away from the car.

He was stunned and winded and had his work shoes in his rucksack, which dug into his back, so he thought he'd damaged his spine. Then he heard it, the sound that fills every bloke who's ever played rugby with dread, "Don't move him, I'm a First Aider." He didn't see his saviour's face, but he was a big lad judging from the size of his backside wedged in Gary's full-face helmet allegedly to stop him from moving his neck. He said a little prayer when he heard the ambulance siren as he was finding it hard to breathe. The weight then moved off his head and he found himself lying in the ambulance being checked over by a paramedic.

Of course, what does he do first, shine a light in Gary's left eye. The panic was on. "I'm getting no response," was shouted and as they began to open his jacket presumably to carry out the cardiac massage, Gary said, "It's false, you silly sod!" He saw the ambulance guy visibly flinch and then take on a sheepish look.

He was taken to the hospital where he was checked out. Apparently, he'd popped something in his spine, but it would heal. His shoes in the rucksack were the cause of the back pain and he was soon discharged to go home.

That evening, Gary was contacted by the uniformed police officer who was dealing with the accident, who he obviously knew. The officer explained that the driver of the car was very sorry, wanted to apologise in person and would it be okay to give him Gary's address. He just said, "Yes, okay, what's his name?" To which he replied, "Thomas Cooper." Gary said, "You're having me on. What's his proper name?" He replied, "Just like that!" He said he'd been waiting all day to get me.

By the way, the other driver's name was really, Thomas Cooper!

Being now office-bound and sitting behind a desk increased his weight considerably. Whilst putting on weight reduced the chances of him being kidnapped by anyone other than an Olympian champion weightlifter, the choice of clothes he could still wear was reducing with every mouthful of food. So, the fat lad decided to get fit and improve his health and no doubt that would also help his mental well-being.

By late 1984 to early 1985 he had finished with his operations and had decided to convert his garage into a makeshift gym. He had a punchbag and weights and a couple of benches.

So, he began firstly going for a run, but he says he thought he probably looked like some broken down old pit pony puffing and panting down the road. However, fortunately for him this time no joint fan of the previously mentioned Ysabel Kid mistook him for such and attempted to bite his ear to calm him!

He could only run about half a mile at first and then had to walk back but as time went on, he was running about five miles each evening. The running coupled with the weights and punchbag in the garage meant he started to lose weight and get fit. All this taken into account he still missed operational police work.

By December of 1988, the Pearsons had their son, aged 7 years, and daughter, who was now three years old. Gary and his wife had taken both to a divisional police Christmas party, not a pleasant experience because with so many excited kids together it was always destined to be bedlam. On the way home at about 8 pm, they were driving through a rough area of Salford when he noticed a signed police car parked at an angle half on the pavement and half on the road, the driver's door was open but no sign of the police officer.

As they started to drive past the police vehicle it could be seen there was a dirt path leading to some houses and there was a vehicle at the bottom of the path that looked to have both rear passenger doors open.

Gary knew something was not right and immediately turned right into a side street, stopped the car and got out. He told his wife, "If this starts to go wrong lock the car and drive home and I'll see you later."

He went quickly to the dirt path and could hear shouting; it sounded like a struggle was in progress. He ran on to the car on the path and saw two men fighting with a policewoman. Gary, whilst shouting, 'Police' because he was in civvies, grabbed the biggest one and bounced his head off the roof of the car, grabbed and bent his arm so far up his back that he yelped out in pain. (The fitness regime had proven beneficial dividends.) He continued to hold him in a forceful arm-lock and saw the second man run towards the houses. The policewoman got out of the car and before he could ask what was happening, he saw about eight men appear from the direction of the houses.

Each one was armed with some sort of weapon. As the policewoman and he were stood between the car and a metal fence they were not easily accessible but a member of the group who was doing most of the shouting moved towards Gary. He says he cannot explain why but he wasn't feeling any fear and weirdly he felt calm.

The man moved towards him and raised his hand whilst holding what looked like a chair leg. He took that gesture to mean that he was about to try to hit him with it. When he got close enough, Gary yelled at him that 'If he tried to attack him, he would snap the arm of the man he was holding and then he would take the weapon from him and put it where the sun didn't shine'. He applied even more pressure to the arm he was holding and the owner yelped even louder than he did before.

Fortunately, like all cowards, the man with the chair leg backed off. Gary then told the policewoman to radio for assistance and within minutes the 'cavalry' arrived in the form of about ten police officers. Gary escorted the man he was holding to a police van and told the officers on the van that the policewoman would deal with him. Gary then returned to his waiting family still in the car and they continued the journey home.

It was some weeks later that he was asked for a witness statement for court, and he ended up going to Crown Court to give evidence but never got a 'talking part'. They decided to plead guilty to theft of a vehicle and assaulting the policewoman.

On Gary's return to work after about two months of being off he was designated an office job. He was far from happy, but he at least had a job and still could pay the mortgage. He had to use a computer a lot and it soon became apparent that his right eye was not ready for that. He seemed to have a constant headache and his eye after a while began to ache and vision was blurred.

He soon ended up with glasses and these did help, and he found he could put up with the headaches and blurred vision. However, what he couldn't put up with but could do nothing about was the attitude of one of the detective inspectors. Gary says that he didn't know if he could sense that he thought the inspector was a useless police officer and in return wanted to belittle him in front of others in the office. He would come into the office greeting people by name but when he saw me, he addressed me as 'Cyclops!' He says initially he was shocked that a senior officer could be so childish, especially when he would turn around to look at the others in the office with a smirk on his face as if looking for a round of applause even though he could see no one else was laughing.

This was a daily occurrence, and it went on for nearly five years. Eventually, one day in 1989 after he had arrived at work and wasn't feeling 100% in that he had a blinding headache, the inspector minced in with his usual salutations and ended with, "Morning, Cyclops."

Gary really wanted to punch him in the face, but he realised that's probably what the big kid wanted, then he would have won, and he'd be left with nothing.

Gary picked up the phone and asked to speak to the now Detective Superintendent Astles, his sergeant when he was in the 'C' Division. Without any preamble, he told Gary to come to headquarters and speak to him which he did that day.

When Gary spoke to him, he had already decided that he was not going to be as childish as the inspector and he was not going to tell tales. What he did say which was true, that his headaches were really bad, and the constant computer work was affecting his vision.

Gary says to give him his due, the detective superintendent just said, "What do you want to do?" Gary just said, "Go." He asked him when and he said, "Now." He said, "I will sort everything," and he did.

Gary left the Greater Manchester Police in 1989.

CHAPTER 8

LIFE AFTER THE POLICE

After leaving the police, Gary, took on the duties of a house husband while his wife worked.

He would take the children to their nearby primary school and pick them up after school and whilst there he would often engage in conversations with some of the mothers who were also bringing and collecting their children. Very soon conversations involved ingredients for curries and other meals.

After about a month of this, his wife came home and asked how his day had gone, and Gary innocently told her he had been discussing making meat pies with some ladies at the school. One of them had told him about using puff pastry and said he could go to her home, and she would show him how she makes her pies and have a coffee. After a short pause, his wife said firmly, "You're getting a job!"

Knowing when he had to do as he was told, that's exactly what Gary did. He saw an advert in the paper asking for applications for the position of Senior Civilian Enforcement officer at Eccles Magistrates' Court, Salford. He applied and was successful.

His duties were to execute warrants issued by the Eccles Magistrates and this meant him driving to the address of a person named on the warrant and bailing them to a future court date.

It soon became apparent that people were getting into trouble because they defaulted on their fines because they didn't even have the money for their bus fare to court.

As he had previously worked in Swinton and Little Hulton whilst in the police, before he was injured, he went to speak to senior officers at Little Hulton to see if he could start a fines' surgery in the police station on a Wednesday from 10 am to 12 noon and again in the afternoon from 5 pm to 7 pm, and they agreed.

He then sent out a standard letter addressed to the person who was named on the warrant stating that he was in possession of a warrant for their arrest and if they attended at Little Hulton police station between the times on the letter he would sort out their problem.

The first Wednesday he opened for business only about 8 or 9 people attended but he decided to stick with it and very soon the police station reception area was crowded with people turning up. Many paid their outstanding fines or payment terms were set up. The scheme was so successful Gary was receiving sometimes in excess of four thousand pounds in cash and the court had to eventually install a safe in the police station.

However, word went around that falsely, Gary, did not have the power to arrest anyone and one afternoon a local idiot came in to speak to him. After a brief conversation he told Gary where he could stick the 'No Bail' warrant he had for him. He asked him if he would just wait while he packed up his paperwork and could discuss the matter fully.

They walked out of the police station and the man was laughing and calling

Gary all the offensive names his tiny brain could think of.

As they got to the car, a beaten-up 405 Peugeot, Gary opened the passenger door and put his paperwork on the seat. He then walked to the rear of the car and after a brief struggle simply put the man in the boot. He drove back to the court building and placed him in a cell. The man was close to tears screaming and shouting what he was going to do to Gary, who struggled to stop laughing as did the cell officer. What made the man worse was the fact that when he appeared before the magistrates, they found his accusations too absurd to be believed!

Gary maintains that if he'd actually been called upon by the magistrates to explain why the man was placed in the boot instead of inside the car, he says that he could have defended his actions, by pointing out that he was on his own, had no way of summoning assistance and being that he had to drive without causing a danger, inside the boot was the safest place for the stroppy individual.

Goodness knows what would have become of the man if the car boot had been full. I dared not enquire if there was a roof rack fitted!

When I questioned Gary about it, he just shrugged and said, "Well, how the hell could I drive and keep one eye on the road and one on him? Don't forget I've only got one eye!"

Gary Pearson sure had his own methods of dealing with awkward folks and situations and many times they worked, to boot!

After about three years of Gary working from Eccles Magistrates' Court it was decided that to save costs, both Eccles and Salford Magistrates' Courts would amalgamate with fewer cases heard at Eccles and the main work being done at Salford Court.

He was told that he would cover both court areas as the senior civilian fines' enforcement officer. He had three enforcement officers who he was responsible for, two female officers and one male officer.

The male officer seemed to Gary the most unlikely enforcement officer he had ever seen. He was always dishevelled in appearance, sometimes looking like he had been dragged through a hedge backwards or had slept in a skip. He came into work one day saying he had hurt his toe and as Gary looked at his foot, he could see he had cut the top of his shoe completely off and his toe was sticking out of the end. He explained that he had done that because the end of his shoe was pressing on his toe.

As he hobbled about in his dishevelled state and now with his one open-toe style shoe, Gary imagined he was in a comedy film working alongside Charlie Chaplin!

He did confide that he didn't like being an enforcement officer and as Gary didn't like him being one either, he came up with an amicable arrangement that satisfied both of them. He managed to get him a good retirement package.

Gary says that was about the only time he got him to 'toe the line,' when he got him the 'boot!'

This now meant that there were only three officers to cover all of the Eccles and Salford areas and in order to get the job done, now a fines' surgery was started at Eccles Police Station, every Thursday between 10 am to 12 noon and 5 pm to 7 pm.

Gary says, 'We had some real characters come into the court and one in particular comes to mind, Vinegar Vera. I first met Vera in the late 1970s when I was in a pub in Salford. I was standing at the bar having a pint when I heard a scream from outside in the street.

I came out of the pub to see what was going on and saw Vera beating up her boyfriend but not wishing to get the same I went back into the pub.

It was now some years later and I was standing in the fines' office in Salford Magistrates' Court when I heard a woman's voice using expletives that would make a docker blush. I looked through the armoured glass into the reception area and saw Vera talking to her friend. It wasn't really the language being used that shocked me it was the fact that Vera had on the shortest skirt and the finishing touch was she was wearing a string vest and no bra.

There are in life some things that people see and can't unsee, this was definitely one of mine.'

It was around 1996 that the civil service took responsibility over the criminal courts in Greater Manchester. The 10 Magistrates' Courts in the Greater Manchester area, Manchester, Salford, Eccles, Bolton, Wigan, Trafford, Tameside, Rochdale, Stockport and Oldham would now be amalgamated into the Ministry of Justice.

After an interview, Gary was promoted to the team leader of the civilian enforcement officers and would now supervise 55 enforcement officers and a warrant office in each one of the 10 courts and their respective staff.

Things, as they say, were taking off. Enforcement officers were now paired up and each pair was equipped with a van containing a secure cell in which to place persons arrested. No longer were officers expected to use their own vehicles. There was also the issue of personal protective equipment, waterproof jackets, mobile phones and even stab vests and training in what powers the officers had.

One of the main frustrations for an enforcement officer was the inability to enter a defendant's property even if they were standing looking out of their window whilst shouting and laughing at the officers.

In 2003 this was to change, the new Courts Act gave officers the power to enter any premises where the officers had reasonable cause to suspect a defendant to be. So, if they went to an address and a defendant refused to open the door, they had the authority to kick the door in. Using these powers was a game changer and the word soon went around that refusal to open the door when asked was not a bar to officers entering.

However, whilst some of the changes were for the better not all were, in that the way the civil service is run can be frustrating. For instance, the waterproof jackets issued to officers were really not substantial enough and tended to rip easily and the zips soon broke. Gary took issue with this and used some of his budget to buy Berghaus jackets which were better quality and even surprisingly cheaper. He received emails informing him that he was not allowed to do this and had to use the suppliers the civil service designates. He didn't.

Gary enjoyed his service in the courts and really showed those who doubted his ability to get on with his life, by not getting bogged down with feeling sorry for himself or wasting time hating what had happened to him. He also enjoyed showing people that if you think you're a victim you will be a victim, and he certainly didn't have time for that self-pity.

During this time Gary's brother, Dean, sadly died of organ failure on 29 October 2009. He was only 53 years of age.

In 2011 the civil service in their infinite wisdom decided to reduce staff to save on budgets but rather than getting rid of some of the more senior members, they opted to, as is frequent in all aspects of occupations, shed the staff that actually did the job. The scheme came out that you could apply for voluntary redundancy. So, Gary did, and he retired.

CHAPTER 9

GARY FULLY RETIRES

Once Gary retired from work altogether, he concentrated all his energy on sorting out his very large house. Although he had installed an oil-fired Esse cooker and boiler it really did struggle to heat the whole house, but he also still had 3 fireplaces that could be used. It now became his mission to collect wood from wherever he could and that soon became known to several arborists who would phone him if they had some logs.

On one occasion Gary received a phone call from a good friend, Fred. The two families had been friends since their children were born. Fred explained that he had just passed a building site, and he had gone in to enquire if he could take the trees they had cut down. He went on to say that the site manager had said, "Yes." As there was a lot of wood to be had Gary hired a lorry for the weekend.

The weekend came but when Fred and Gary arrived at the site no one was present, and it was surrounded by security fencing. It was a simple job to open up one of the panels to access the wood and once that had been done, they started loading the lorry. They had loaded about half the wood when a signed police vehicle arrived.

That first police vehicle was joined shortly after by another 3 patrol vehicles, 2 vans and a dog van. This was fast turning into a scene from a farce and if it hadn't been so serious Gary might have thought he was in a comedy sketch with the punchline being that the next police unit to turn up would be... Special Branch!

A policewoman walked over to the pair and asked what they were doing. Gary told her that the site manager had given Fred permission to remove the wood and looked at Fred, who oddly didn't look back at Gary but instead he chose to look at his shoes and the ground.

The policewoman was adamant that they were 'nicking' the wood but Gary thinks he'd almost convinced her of their innocence until Gary and Fred's sons arrived with the chainsaws, which seemed to change her mind.

As the police officers opened the rear of the police van to put Gary and Fred in another police vehicle arrived and out stepped a police officer whom Gary had spent some years working with in the Tactical Aid Group. Clutching at straws, Gary immediately shouted to him and asked him to let the other officers know that he wasn't a thief. The police officers walked off a few paces to obviously discuss Gary and Fred's fate.

Then the policewoman came back to them and told Gary and Fred they could go. Gary later asked Fred if the site manager had given permission to take the wood, to which Fred replied, "Well he didn't exactly say so, but he also didn't say, no." Gary's association with Fred would later only get worse, whereby he would have a fully automatic rifle pointed at him!

One afternoon Fred rang Gary and asked if he fancied going to a new Cajun restaurant that had just opened in Manchester. Gary said okay and later that evening they met up and had a great meal and some lovely wine.

As they were leaving Gary suggested they get a taxi home, but Fred was adamant they should take the Metrolink, which is Manchester's tram system. Gary had never been on it and neither had Fred. They walked to Victoria station where they knew they could catch a tram.

Inside the station, they didn't have a clue as to where they could buy a ticket, but they saw a large freestanding machine with Metrolink written on the side, so they went to that. It was apparent that they could purchase the tickets there but unfortunately, it wasn't lit up. They tried putting money in it, but it looked like it wasn't working. A young chap who could see they were struggling went over to them. He said that the machine was out of order.

After last travelling on a train when he was perhaps 20 years old or so, Gary remembered paying the ticket man whilst he was on the train and so he just said to Fred that they'd pay on the tram.

After waiting on the platform for a short time a tram arrived and they got on it, it was very full, and they stood by a door. According to the rail plan on the tram wall, they were about 3 stops from their destination and as Gary looked down the tram, he could see a man in a fluorescent jacket checking tickets and by the time he got to them, Gary had his wallet out ready to pay.

The ticket checker asked for their tickets and Gary explained that the machine at Victoria station was broken so he wished to pay him for 2 tickets from Victoria to Bury. He stared at Gary for a couple of seconds then without saying a word he walked back down the tram from where he had come.

Minutes later Gary looked down the tram and could see 6 police officers walking up the tram and he said to Fred, "Looks like someone's in trouble." However, they stopped when they got to Gary and Fred and behind them was the ticket checker. Gary says, 'Now I'm not very tall, about 5'10" but these uniformed officers were quite small, and they looked about 5'4" but they had police uniforms on'. They asked Gary and

Fred for their tickets, and they were also told that the ticket machine at Victoria station was broken but they thought they could pay on the tram.

At this, the ticket checker shouted that the machine was not broken. The young chap who was at the station who had told them it wasn't working came forward to confirm that it was broken. One of the officers pushed the chap against the door of the tram and put his arm up his back. At this, Fred said to Gary, "Let's deck them." Gary could see the treatment of the young chap had agitated him but told him to wait as he didn't think this was going to end well and as it turned out it didn't.

At the next station, the tram stopped the door opened and on the platform was a full section of TAG police officers, 10 constables and a sergeant but they were not armed. The officers on the train had obviously phoned for assistance in case the 2 suited geriatrics kicked off. The TAG officers escorted Gary and Fred off the tram and along the platform to the main road where their van could be seen.

When they were on the road, Gary turned to the sergeant and asked if he did not feel embarrassed to be arresting two old blokes who had never travelled on the tram before and just thought it was like travelling on a train. Gary also disclosed that he was a retired police officer, and he had been one of the first officers in TAG in 1977.

The sergeant gave the TAG constables a nod and they walked off to their van. It's thought that they probably got a call from Metrolink saying there was trouble on a tram only to see that there was not. So then, Fred and Gary found themselves left about 3 miles from Bury and so they hailed a cab, which dropped them off at a pub near Bury bus station.

Gary said he would phone his wife to come and get them but before he did, they went into the pub for a pint. One pint then led to another, and they had been brought to the attention of two ladies who were out for the evening and so they ended up chatting to them and of course, more beer was drunk. Thinking he best phone his wife before he lost the power of sensible speech, Gary phoned her and explained where they were and asked her to phone him when she was outside.

After some time, Gary's phone rang so Fred and he staggered out but couldn't immediately see his wife. It seems when hitting the outside fresh air, the beer took over and Gary's ability to walk evaporated. Strangely enough, it seemed that way with Fred too and they had to hang onto one another to stop from falling over.

It was then that Gary heard his wife shout, "Are you 2 Freddie Frinton's getting in this car?" How they managed to walk to the car Gary has no idea, and it didn't help his wife's mood having 2 highly dressed-up women shouting and waving, 'Bye-bye' to Fred and Gary. It took Gary's wife a while for her to forgive and forget this if she ever has!

NOTE. Freddie Frinton (Born: 17 January 1909, Grimsby. Died: 16 October 1968 age 59 years), was a famous and popular English comedian, music hall and television actor. He is primarily remembered today as being a household name during his era and a big part of his act was his portrayal of a drunk.

Gary and Fred are members of an order which is known as The Honourable Order of Bass Drinkers, the order meets on the first Monday of the month where they drink copious amounts of draught Bass and Gary describes that they 'speak in broken biscuits'.

I have to confess that I hadn't heard of the saying to 'speak in broken biscuits' until now, so I had to look it up and found it means: 'Speak in broken biscuits' is a British idiom that means to speak in a way that is unclear or broken.

It was at one such meeting that the decision was made to visit Prague and whilst there Gary, Fred and the group would visit their magnificent brewery. The day arrived and they all met at Manchester airport and were soon on their way to a magnificent hotel situated right in the middle of the city.

The first day Gary and Fred spent the time walking around the many beautiful buildings and sampling the wonderful stews, but they decided the following day they would try and look further afield. When they got back to the hotel, Gary went to reception to find out what the best transport would be for the trip the next day. The receptionist said they should buy a ticket that covered both the bus and the underground services.

The following day, Gary once again enquired at reception where would be the best place to buy the travel tickets and the receptionist was able to point to a small wooden hut opposite the hotel and said they could get them there. So, buying 2 one-day tickets, they were set and decided on travelling by bus as they could then hop off if they saw something worth viewing more closely.

Once again, they visited lots of places and helped to get rid of several pints of Czech beer and probably too much of their famous stews. It was Fred who decided they should travel back to the hotel using the underground as it would be quicker. So off they went to the nearest station and boarded a train. It didn't take long to get back to the station near their hotel, so they got off and began walking down the platform.

They hadn't walked far when they were approached by a rather dishevelled individual who took hold of Gary's arm and spoke in Czech, but he didn't have a clue what he was saying. Gary took hold of his hand, pulled it off his and pushed him away. He said to Fred that he thought he was begging but the man persisted in standing in front of Gary and holding his hands up to Gary's chest.

Gary was getting a bit annoyed by now and thought the man could see this from his face. The scruffy man then beckoned to 3 very heavily armed police officers who were standing at the base of the stairs leading up to the street and the hotel and they walked over. The man then came out with this torrent in Czech and kept indicating to Gary and Fred. Eventually one of the officers spoke, while the other 2 stood on each side of them, with their fully automatic weapons pointed very closely in their direction.

The officer speaking very good English stated the man who Gary thought was begging was the ticket checker. Gary had an instantaneous flash of 'Deja Vu' but then he knew there was no problem because this time he had bought the tickets. He took the tickets out of his pocket and waved them under the ticket checker's nose with a grin, but the man looked disappointed. He took the tickets from Gary and looked at them and then the little ticket checker/toad said something to the officer, and he was now smiling. The officer explained that whilst they had bought tickets, they had not had them validated. Gary asked him how you do that, and he told him that near every 'In' going turnstile there was a cigarette packet-sized device that you must put the ticket through, and this stamped a validation date.

The officer then told Gary and Fred they were to go with them to a room at the side where they would have to pay a large fine and the ticket checker would issue a receipt. When they got in the room the ticket checker asked the officer to tell Gary and Fred that the fine would be 300 kroner. Gary says he was shocked at the size of the fine considering it could be seen that they bought tickets.

He was even more shocked when Fred started laughing and he produced a roll of banknotes that would have 'choked a donkey' and peeled off 6 x 100 kroner notes. The 'toad' and the officers were as equally shocked as Gary. When Fred and Gary got out of the station and were walking to the hotel, Gary asked Fred why he laughed, and he just said a fine of about £10 each was a winner and to see the ticket checker's face was a bonus!

Gary says he now enjoys his relaxed retirement with his wife and family who live nearby. He has an interest in vintage cars. He enjoys wine tasting and is a member of a number of clubs for folks with a similar passion. He says he really loves cooking and especially for his family including the grandkids, who all arrive without fail at what is referred to as 'Grandpa's Cafe' every Sunday morning.

Grandpa Gary is in his element in his regular role as duty breakfast chef when the 4 parents and 4 grandkids drop by to join Grandpa and Grandma Pearson for a full English breakfast, bacon sarnie, 'skinheads on a raft' or whatever takes your fancy.

It looks like the Pearson/Leyland tradition of a Sunday get-together for a meal continues and I hope that 'Grandpa's Cafe' remains open for business for many more years to come.

Now we return to the more serious matter of the 'Cold Case Review.'

CHAPTER 10

COLD CASE REVIEW

(Carried out by Kevin Moore and separately by Tom Curry.)

GARY PEARSON'S WITNESS STATEMENT

Great Manchester Police.

Statement of Witness.

(C.J. Act 1967, ss 2,9; M.C. Rules, 158.)

Statement of Gary Ralph Pearson. Age of witness 3. 8. 53. Tel. No. 773-7537.

Occupation of witness Police Constable 'F' 1808.

Address 35 Farm Lane Simister Nr. Prestwich.

Taken by: Det. Ch. Insp. James. 8.12.83. Time: 3.15 pm.

I am a Police Officer in the Greater Manchester Police currently am undertaking foot patrol duties at Swinton 'F' Division. I have eleven and a half years police service, having joined the service in 1972. I have been an authorised firearms officer for five years having passed a basic course in 1978. During that five years I have progressed in the proficiency of firearms to advanced level which is the top grading any officer can achieve with this.

In the last two years I have been seconded to the firearms department for periods of approximately six months on two separate occasions to assist the staff in that department in the training of Saudi Arabian and other overseas students on firearm courses.

Although I have only been seconded in the capacity of an aide. I am very conversant with the system of training students in the use of firearms and of the safety measures which need to be employed.

Page 1

On every occasion a student is under instruction.

I also consider myself to be a very capable officer in the police use of firearms required in an operational situation. During both secondments I have taken part in many such operations and on several occasions, I have been a member of the main arrest team.

In August 1983 I was asked by Detective Chief Inspector James if I would be willing to be seconded to his department for a period of three months to assist with the training of Saudi Arabian and Bahrain Police officers provided, I would be spared from my division. I was most willing to agree to this request and the necessary arrangements were put in hand. I commenced my secondment as an aide in the firearms department on the 15th of August 1983 and I have assisted in the firearms training of these students throughout their course, but I am not a qualified firearms instructor.

On Sunday 13th November 1983, together with Detective Constable Milner I travelled to Bailey Head pursuit centre in Cumbria and my responsibility would be to assist that officer in training Saudi Arabian and Bahrain officers in VIP ambush and anti-ambush techniques. The groups of students numbered 10 in all.

Late in the afternoon on that day I was present with Detective Constable Milner and gave a practical demonstration and lecture to all the students in relation to the dangers of using wax bullets and blank ammunition. He claimed that the weapons when fired should never be pointed directly at a person and the effects of doing so was clearly shown on sheets of paper which

Page 2

were holed and shredded at the conclusion of the demonstration.

The following day Monday 14th November 1983, I accompanied the group of students and Milner on outside-line armed exercises. During these exercises wax bullets are used by the students in their Smith and Wesson revolvers. And the exercises were a complete success. A number of shots were fired by the students but only as instructed there was no occasion when any student had acted inappropriately in the use of their respective weapons on the discharge of rounds.

On Tuesday 15th November 1983, the exercises related to anti- ambush, ambush and V.I.P protection duties and on that morning, I am of the opinion that only wax bullets were issued to the students. I was not responsible for the issue of rounds and that task was undertaken by Detective Constable Milner I was not present when the issue took place. There were several exercises that morning in (? unable to read) and once again these exercises were successful with no improper use by either weapons or ammunition.

Once these exercises were completed, we all returned to the pursuit centre for lunch about 12:15 pm. I was aware that Milner collected ammunition for the students which had not been used but once again I did not take part in that procedure as I was busy doing other duties.

After lunch we left the pursuit centre to continue with similar exercises in the same location. Police Constable Mitchell a force firearms instructor had arrived during lunch from Manchester, and he had brought with him a supply of blank ammunition and on leaving

Page 3

the pursuit centre Milner took this supply with him in the personal carrier in which I accompanied him. The supply of blank ammunition was retained in a cardboard box and brown envelope and although I did not specifically inspect the contents in the box, I know the system of storing blank ammunition was that separate different calibres are stored together and utilised as and when distributed by the instructor in charge of the particular exercise.

When we reached the forest, as Milner was the instructor he handed out the required rounds of blank ammunition to each student. My duties kept me busy with preparation matters and I did not see him actually hand the rounds to the students. We went through about three exercises that afternoon and then the majority of that time I was in a separate part of the forest from Milner. We only came together for the final exercise about three o'clock and I was present with Milner when he briefed six students.

They were told the exercise was for observation and concealment and I was conscious of the selected students coming to Milner to be replenished with rounds. I cannot remember the exact names of all the six selected students, but I know that Zaffir Mispha and a Bahraini were amongst the group. When briefed and ready the students set off to prepare for the exercise and the vehicles, we left on a pre-arranged route through the forest. I was in the front passenger seat of the lead vehicle driven by Milner and Sergeant Lofthus was in the vehicle behind us with the remaining students.

In travelling the route, I saw Zaffir throw a part of a tree.

Page 4

across the road to block our path and the other five students had taken up various positions in the same locality as we came to a stop, I heard shooting, and such the shooting had ceased. Milner signalled to the students that the exercise was over, at that time I saw Zaffir approach the front of the vehicle and fire two or three blank rounds from a distance of fifteen yards clear to a distance very close to the front of the vehicle Zaffir then went to the driver's window and I saw him lift his revolver whilst no more than a few inches from the driver's window and fire the weapon.

There was then an immediate loud explosion whereby the driver's and the passenger's windows were shattered, and I witnessed extreme pain to the left side of my head and face about my eye I could tell immediately that I was very badly injured and I together with Milner who had also been injured was rushed to hospital at Carlisle. As a consequence, this injury my left eye has been removed and fragments of metal are still present in the socket itself. I also experience pain and discomfort on a regular day to day basis and I have a wound beneath the eye likely to require plastic surgery.

In my opinion the ability of the students on this particular overseas course starts from poor to very good but at all times all students have to be closely accompanied.

In the afternoon exercise one student was remonstrated with by Milner for discharging his weapon to close to the driver's window of the vehicle driven by Sergeant Lofthus and the excess powder on the window was pointed out to the whole group to show the dangers of such a practice.

Page 5

I was issued of the safety glasses at the armoury store for use in firearms training, but they would not have been suitable in this particular location and would in the circumstances have been ineffective.

I know Milner extremely well and I consider him to be the most confident firearms instructor on the current department staff. I feel certain he would never make a mistake in issuing a wrong calibre round and I can only think that the rounds have at some time been accessible to the students and they have helped themselves.

In my opinion the accident was probably caused by a .32 blank being inserted into a chamber followed by a .38 blank in the same chamber which has caused the .32 to be discharged like a bullet without a head. This is based on the fact that it is within my knowledge that the remains of a .32 blank case have been found in the damaged vehicle.

This statement was written in the presence of Mr Aubrey Isaacson @ 49 King Street, Manchester.

FIREARMS EXPERT'S REPORT: DATED 11 APRIL 1985 COMMISSIONED BY GARY PEARSON

COLIN GREENWOOD

FIREARMS RESEARCH & ADVISORY SERVICE

Report Re: G.R. PEARSON

Colin GREENWOOD, aged 52, firearms consultant of Broadstone Farm, Colden, Hebden Bridge, West Yorkshire HX7 7PH.

Qualifications.

I am in business as a firearms consultant. I have been concerned with the study of firearms over thirty years. I have been involved with all types of shooting including games shooting with shotgun and rifle, clay pigeon shooting, competitive rifle and pistol shooting at national and international level. I have held various police national championships and have shot for Great Britain in the European Police Championships.

I have completed twenty-five years police service and retired in December 1979 with the rank of Superintendent. During my police service I was responsible for the design and implementation of a system of firearms training in West Yorkshire Police which was subsequently adopted by many other forces. I was in charge of firearms training for a number of years and was concerned with the making of recommendations on police training and police weaponry at national level. I have been closely involved in technical research into weapon selection and ammunition performance. I specified the design of rifles and shotguns which have been adopted in many parts of the country. I have conducted tests extensively into the performance of rifle and pistol ammunition and have been involved in research in the performance of body armour and other bullet resistant materials.

I have advised police forces in various parts of the world on aspects of firearms training, weapons selection and related subjects. I was the only person outside of the United States to contribute to a U.S. bureau of standards research project into police pistol ammunition. I have advised the New Zealand Government in the selection of police rifles. I have lectured widely to police officers of all ranks on firearms and related subjects. I am the authors of three books on police training, tactics and weaponry and have written a large number of articles on these subjects in a wide range of journals.

I am the Editor of the monthly magazine Guns Review and 1 contribute to a number of other magazines on various topics related to firearms. I regularly examine and review new weapons of all classes and report on them for the magazine which I edit and for other magazines. In my capacity as a firearms consultant, I am retained by a number of manufacturers and importers of firearms who consult me on matters relating to firearms control and weapons design.

I have given evidence at Magistrates' and Crown Courts in a large number of cases involving the technical aspects of firearms, ammunition performance and the development and application of firearms law. As long ago as 1967 I was commended by the Director of Public Prosecutions for my expertise in cases involving firearms.

In 1969 I was awarded a Research Fellowship at the University of Cambridge Institute of Criminology to study the development of firearms control and their effects on armed crime, accidents and suicides. As part of my research, I studied the development of the law relating to firearms including the background situations which led to the legislation all Government and Departmental Studies and Reports, all primary and secondary legislation passed in the country, all debates in both House of Parliament, together with comments and submissions made by various bodies in respect of legislation on firearms. The result of this work was subsequently published as a book FIREARMS CONTROL (Routledge & Kegan Paul, London 1972). The book has been accepted as an authoritative work on the subject and has been quoted and accepted as persuasive argument in Crown Court. Since completing my research fellowship, I have continued research in this field and produced a number of smaller studies published in various journals.

In connection with firearms legislation, I have been consulted by the Home Affairs Committee and both major political parties in this country and have advised various official, sporting and trade bodies. I have lectured widely in this country to various official groups, sporting and trade organisations. I have attended international conferences and seminars in the United States, Australia and New Zealand as a Speaker. I have advised on the drafting of legislation and the probable effects of specific proposals. I have contributed to legal and sporting journals in a number of countries on various aspects of firearms legislation.

Report

The conduct of exercises in police firearms training requires a great deal of careful preparation. Unless the exercises have a considerable degree of realism, they will be devoid of any stress and will not achieve their purpose. If exercises are carefully planned, it is possible to create the sort of stress which will cause quite remarkable reactions. I have on a number of occasions, seen men "break" under the stress of carefully designed and mounted exercises.

To achieve that sort of effect it is necessary that blank cartridges which create about the same noise level as a live round should be used. The noise of a gun being fired close by, particularly indoors, is very loud and creates a pronounced physic al effect on a person under stress. It is vital that officers undergoing firearms training are subjected to these stresses.

9. In the course of the training programmes I devised for the West Yorkshire Police, a number of exercises were mounted for all students. Different and more complex exercises were mounted for student instructors and for specialise training. In all of them, blank cartridges were used and in some of them wax bullets were used. The latter consists of a standard cartridge case in which the flash hole has been enlarged. This is loaded with a small 'bullet' of paraffin wax and a primer.

10. Wax bullets for use in the exercises were made by instructors. To ensure that the cartridge cases were easily recognised a large notch was cut into the base with a file.

11. Commercially available blank cartridges for the .38 revolvers are usually sealed by means of a card wadding and a sealant. Tests conducted with targets and card, wood and saturated newspapers (which create a rough approximation to soft flesh) indicate that these card wads could cause serious injuries at close range. The risk involved was considered unacceptable and arrangements were made to load blanks within the department. A special die was made to close the blanks with a coning which obviated the need for wad closure. This was a simple process, and the equipment needed, apart from the special die, was both readily available and inexpensive.

12. The procedure adopted in the exercises was as follows. Those participants who would be using their firearms were required to step out in front of the syndicate and, one at once, each loaded their pistols showing each blank cartridge or wax bullet to the person at whom they might be firing, in the presence of the remainder of the syndicate. Each person involved was then searched by his "opponent" to ensure that he had no other ammunition of any sort. Any additional blank ammunition was removed from the scene. No reloading was permitted.

13. This procedure was rigidly imposed and was repeated as each new exercise started. At the end of each exercise, those involved were required to unload in the presence of the entire syndicate and show their unloaded pistol to all involved. Each time a pistol was taken from the holster it had to be broken and shown to all those present at the exercise. The procedure was strictly adhered to during the whole of my time in the Firearms Training and continued after I left. It is still strictly enforced.

14. Although the procedure was an inconvenience at times, it was regarded as part of the overall safety training. Safety with firearms must become a matter of habit and it was required that a weapon should be "proved" each time it was taken from a holster or picked up, even though that weapon might have holstered only a moment or so before. The most

rigorous action was taken in respect of any failure to follow safety rules stringently. On one occasion student instructors were delivering final lectures in a classroom at the end of a twelve-week course. When one of them failed to "prove" a pistol with which he was demonstrating a point, he was removed from the course at once, despite the fact that this meant that 12 weeks had been wasted. It was considered that no allowance could be made for anyone in matters relating to safety. Once that attitude had been established, problems with safety simply did not arise.

15. Even with the crimp closure, blank cartridges can cause injury. A small number of powder burns occurred, and, in such cases, small particles of powder might be embedded in the skin. Such incidents were accepted because of the need to generate realism. However, because of the danger, safety glasses were provided for all taking part and added protection was provided for all those at whom wax bullets might be fired.

16. I have read the account provided by Mr. Pearson about the behaviour of certain of the Saudi Arabian students on the course. I can say that such behaviour should not have been tolerated and the person concerned with, for example, unsafe behaviour with a shotgun should have been removed from the course at once. Safety in this sort of training depends on the attitude of the staff and, although it may be inconvenient or unpopular, safety standards must be inflexibly enforced, and a great deal of effort must be put into openly stating and restating that attitude.

17. The attitude on the firearms training courses which I design was carefully designed to create what was called a "sudden death" approach. Many of the normal disciplinary standards of police training were deliberately stopped. For example, students were not required to stand when staff lecturers entered a room, and a very relaxed attitude between staff and students was deliberately engendered. Against that was set the attitudes towards safety. Any failure of safety standards resulted in immediate dismissal from the course with no enquiry and no possibility of

excuse. The entire approach was designed to impress on students and the responsibility for safety rested with them and that any mistake could lead to a sudden death when excuses would be of no value.

18. That approach is, in my view, an essential part of a carefully prepared firearms training programme and any acceptance of lesser standards of safety at any time is almost bound to lead to an accident at some other time. The importance of safety will have been irrecoverably devalued if unsafe conduct is tolerated to the slightest extent.

19. It is clear from the account given by Mr. Pearson that safety standards were extremely lax and when this is coupled with the known attitude of the students, those in charge were seriously at fault.

20. From my experience with blank cartridges, both wadded and crimped. I can say that it is highly unlikely that a blank alone would break a toughened glass window unless the muzzle of the gun was pressed hard on the glass. In this case the surgeon indicates that metallic fragments which he refers to as parts of a primer, are present in the wound. It is not likely that the primer from a blank could have bene projected. Mr. Pearson suggests that a .32 blank might have been loaded into a .38 revolver ahead of the .38 blank but there is no evidence to support this. A .32 blank will fall into the chamber of a .38 revolver until stopped by the forcing cone at the front of the cylinder. In most revolvers it will protrude so far forward that, if the gun is pointed downwards at any time, the cylinder will not revolve. The theory represents a possibility, but no more than that.

21. The availability of cartridges of differing calibres is a serious breach of safety rules. Accidents from that cause are relatively common and every book on shotgun shooting mentions the hazard of having 20 bore cartridges when a 12-bore gun is used. A 20-bore cartridge will slip into a chamber of a 12-bore gun down to the forcing cone. The subsequent

loading and firing of a 12-bore cartridge causes a gun to blow up.

22. The effect of firing a .38 blank behind a .32 blank is not known. It is unlikely that the revolver would blow up, though there could well be some bulging. It would be extremely important that the gun and the cartridges used should be preserved. The police officers concerned can have had no way of knowing whether or not Mr. Pearson would die. At the time of the accident, they therefore had a duty to preserve the exhibits which might be vital in any subsequent enquiry. The exhibits should have been subject to Forensic examination. Tests of the barrel would show the brass deposits which must have been present if a .32 blank had been fired. Examination of the gun might well show signs of over-pressure. I suggest that attempts be made to discover any evidence on this point which is available. If no such action was taken the police officers were most certainly negligent in their duty.

23. It seems highly desirable that tests should be conducted with a similar pistol and similar ammunition to determine the effects of firing a .38 blank behind a .32 blank. It would also be desirable to fire a gun loaded in this way through the window of a Ford Transit van at some target which will give an indication of the striking energy.

24. It is just possible that the window of the vehicle was broken by the blast of the blank cartridge when the muzzle was pressed hard onto the glass. In that case one would expect that fragments of glass would be present in and around the wound. Mr. Orton's report does not mention the state of the wound at the time of admission to hospital as it may be that a statement from the doctor who first saw Mr. Pearson is important. If this second hypothesis is shown to be more likely, the fragment of metal could be from the ruptured .38 blank and a .32 blank may not have featured.

25. It seems to me that efforts should be made to establish, if possible,

exactly how the injury was caused. The weapon itself should still be available for examination as should the cartridges recovered from it. Doubtless the vehicle will have been repaired, but photographs should have been taken should be available. I suggest that I should examine these items and then conduct independent tests indicated above.

26. From the accounts given it seems that the instructors were inside the police vehicles and that the students were unsupervised at the time of the "ambush". That point could perhaps be clarified. If that were so there was yet another failure of normal supervision of students.

Colin Greenwood

11th April 1985

KEVIN MOORE'S CONCLUSIONS

It is generally accepted that a case becomes cold when all viable leads in an investigation have been exhausted, and the Senior Investigating Officer (SIO) considers there is nothing further that can be progressed in the investigation at that time.

Cold Cases are reviewed to determine if any leads have not been followed up correctly and/or newer technologies or forensic testing may produce any new potential leads.

A former colleague, Sussex Police Detective Chief Superintendent Kevin Moore, was the senior investigating officer (SIO) in many murder and major crime cases. He has also reviewed many 'cold cases.'

I approached him to give his professional opinion after viewing the limited evidence of the Gary Pearson injury incident. This he kindly agreed to and here are his findings:

----

1. As there was little available at this time to read, I have already read and considered what has been provided. These consisted of:

Two newspaper articles written by Steve Panter

Statement of Colin Greenwood

Statement of Gary Pearson

2. What I would say right at the outset is that this was a poorly conducted investigation in my opinion with a total lack of appropriate lines of investigation having been conducted. Whilst I appreciate that there may well be other documentation available, the statement of Colin Greenwood suggests that no forensic examination work or test firing of the weapon used in this case has been undertaken. Why this was not done I can only surmise or speculate. It may have been determined at the outset as a decision had already been taken to attribute what took place as being the result of an 'accident'.

3. Mention is also made in the statement of Greenwood that there was no medical evidence available from the medical staff originally treating Gary Pearson. I say this because no evidence is available as regards the nature of the wound caused and the potential for there to be glass fragments if an 'explosion' was caused if the gun was against the glass window of the van door when the shot was discharged.

4. Crucially, the statement of Greenwood is clearly very critical of the lack of compliance with the necessary safety guidance in relation to firearms training. He is therefore directing this towards both Henry Milner as well as Gary Pearson himself. Pearson was of course an aide at the time and was not it would appear a qualified/trained firearms instructor albeit he

was a proficient firearms officer. This could be important because arguably he should not have been training totally inexperienced and untrained individuals in the use of firearms. This may explain why Greater Manchester Police were reluctant to expose this case to greater scrutiny via any potential judicial process.

5. I now come to the incident itself.

6. I have then considered the law in respect of assault occasioning grievous bodily harm with intent S.18 of the Offences Against the Person Act 1861 and S.20 of the Offences Against the Person Act 1861.

7. I do not consider the potential for an offence of attempted murder to be relevant due to the lack of the appropriate mens rea i.e. state of mind of the suspect when the potential offence took place.

8. It is useful to see what the law says at this point in respect of:

Unlawful wounding/inflicting grievous bodily harm.

Section 20 OAPA 1861 – maximum 5 years imprisonment.

GBH means really serious harm. The harm does not have to be either permanent or dangerous: Golding [2014] EWCA Crim 889. Proof of wounding requires a break in the continuity of the skin. The distinction between a section 18 and section 20 GBH is the mens rea of the offence. Charge selection must address the question of recklessness and intention. It is therefore of critical importance, and good practice, to explain how the evidence in the case directly supports recklessness and intention. For a section 20 GBH, the suspect must intend, or foresee, that the act might cause some harm: R v Savage; DPP v Parmenter [1992] 1 AC 699. It is not possible to attempt this offence because in order to attempt it, the consequence (wounding or GBH) must be intended, which is an offence contrary to section 18 instead. The indictment should make clear whether it is wounding or GBH which is alleged.

Indictable-only offences

The following offences triable only in the Crown Court carry a maximum sentence of life imprisonment.

Wounding/causing grievous bodily harm with intent.

Section 18 OAPA 1861

The definition of GBH is as above. This offence (section 18 OAPA 1861) however can only be committed where GBH (or wounding) is intended. It bears repeating that the explanation for the charge selection should directly address the question of recklessness or intention, demonstrating how the evidence in the case supports the decision. Evidence of intention may come from different sources, of which the following are a few examples:

selection and use of a particular weapon

severity or duration of attack

making prior threats or planning a serious attack

relevant admissions in the interview

If section 20 is a possible alternative verdict to section 18, it is good practice for it to appear on the indictment: Lahaye [2005] EWCA Crim 2847 (and in these circumstances, there should be a clear rationale to explain why the prosecution case is that the defendant intended GBH/wounding, why a plea to section 20 is not an acceptable alternative, but that this is a trial issue for the jury to determine).

An offence contrary to section 18 may also be committed where the victim is wounded or caused grievous bodily harm in the course of the defendant resisting or preventing the lawful apprehension of any person. This offence may be used where the injuries amount to grievous bodily harm or injury but where the intention to resist or prevent a lawful apprehension is clearer than the intent to cause a wound or grievous bodily harm.

9. Therefore, the guilt or otherwise of the subject Zaffir Mispha depends very much on what was in his mind at the time that he fired the weapon at the glass window. Was it a deliberate act to cause fear of harm or was it some kind of bizarre prank that went wrong? We are at a massive disadvantage because at this time we don't know if Mispha was interviewed either under caution or not. If he was and there is a record of the interview available, then this would assist considerably. However, without his personal account, we are in great difficulty.

10. I do not believe that consideration of an offence committed under section 18 is relevant for similar reasons as to a case of attempted murder not being appropriate. This is because a very similar state of mind on the part of the subject is necessary in the case of a section 18 offence as is the case for attempted murder. There would need to be proof that there was an intention to cause really serious bodily harm at the time that the act was undertaken.

11. In order to prove recklessness even in the case of a section 20 wounding we need to prove that some form of assault was intended, and I would have to say based on what is available evidentially at this time, that this is not possible to establish. We would need to prove that the subject Mispha had deliberately loaded the weapon with a round or rounds in such a way with the intention to bring about the outcome that occurred or was reckless as to whether it would or not. Again, the evidence available is insufficient at this time to indicate one way or the other.

12. The apparent lack of forensic investigation means we really have no idea evidentially why what happened in terms of the injuries to Gary

Pearson did in fact occur i.e. we don't know and probably never will know what round or rounds were fired. By this, I mean whether there was a .32 calibre wax bullet as well as a .38 blank round in the chamber or just one round of either type/calibre. It could of course have been the case that the weapon itself malfunctioned for some reason although revolvers are relatively straightforward weapons.

Conclusion:

13. In my professional opinion, the whole thing is totally unsatisfactory and frustrating due to there being so many unanswered questions. This is entirely due to what appears to be a poorly conducted or even a lack of a serious investigation into this incident. The question in my mind is simply this. Why was this the case? Of course, this is alluded to in the newspaper articles where the journalist points out the fragile relations between the British and Saudi Arabian Governments that existed at this time.

If there is additional information or evidence forthcoming, then I would be happy to consider this in due course.

Kevin Moore BA (Hons); PgD; Retired Detective Chief Superintendent, Sussex Police.

TOM CURRY'S CONCLUSIONS

Greater Manchester Police (GMP) is the UK police force responsible for law enforcement within the metropolitan county of Greater Manchester in northwest England.

Here are the staff figures for Greater Manchester Police in 1983: Constables: 8,550, including 183 special constables. Police Community

Support Officers: 600.

Greater Manchester Police (GMP) is one of the largest policing areas in England and Wales, covering almost 500 square miles. It has a team of more than 12,000 people, including police officers, non-uniformed staff, and volunteers.

As of 2015, there were 1009 former GMP injured on-duty (IOD) police officers who had subsequently been medically retired due to those sustained injuries and in receipt of an injury pension award. There were a total 15,835 IOD's in England, Wales and Northern Ireland. GMP had the 3rd highest number of IOD's with the Metropolitan Police having the highest of 3283 and the second being Northern Ireland Police with 2566.

I do not have the staffing or IOD figures for the current time.

Sir Cyril James Anderton CBE KStJ QPM DL (24 May 1932 – 5 May 2022) served as chief constable of Greater Manchester from 1976 to 1991.

The shooting of Police Constable Gary Pearson occurred over 40 years ago in 1983 and was a harrowing and tragic incident to say the least. Therefore, it is no surprise that now we find that only the scantest of corroboration evidence is available due to the lengthy passage of time.

At this precise moment that evidence only amounts to the newspaper article which appeared in the Manchester Evening News, Gary's witness statement and Mr Greenwood the firearms expert's report.

The only other witness, Detective Constable Henry Milner is sadly no longer available, he having died in 2020.

Firstly, I will deal with the news article. One has to wonder how reliable that is because the incident occurred on 15 November 1983 and the article is dated 29 January 1991, a lengthy 7+ years after the event. Therefore, how much credibility can we put on it being an accurate account given the time-lapse and it being a mere newspaper article?

What does appear to be the case is that there is no evidence at this stage that it was ever challenged by either Greater Manchester Police (GMP) or anyone else. One has to believe that if it were not true, then as damning as it is, surely GMP and indeed the government would have demanded it be corrected. There is no available evidence of such counter-action.

We have no evidence of the reporter, Steve Panter, seeking corroboration of his claim of a GMP and government cover-up. We have to consider if that was sought and if it were not, then I suggest that would be extremely reckless reporting on his part. As would be the printing by Manchester Evening News alleging such an unsubstantiated, serious and damning claim. In consideration of those it was directed at that would have been likely asking for trouble, I would have thought.

Unless we find evidence to the contrary, we must consider the news article does have some merit but all the time remembering the old newspaper adage of, 'Never let the truth get in the way of a good story'.

Right now, I do not think we can say any more about the news report.

UPDATE

On Friday, 4 October 2024, Steve Panter the author of the Manchester News article rang me. Albeit done 33 years ago, Steve stands by his article's credibility, although he was not able to offer any further information as to his verification checks. We must of course take into account that his reporting is historic, and time will dull recall.

Apparently, all such features must be authorised by the newspaper lawyers and the same policy is still followed to this day.

We move next to Gary's witness statement, which was made 33 days after the incident and whilst he was still recovering from his catastrophic injury. It was written down by Detective Chief Inspector James in the presence of Mr Aubrey Isaacson at the solicitor's office.

I cannot help but try to imagine the state of poor Gary's mind at that time during his early recovery and the trauma he would still be suffering. Of course, we will never know the stress he was experiencing given what he had and was still going through. All I am saying is that we must consider that his mental condition could not have possibly been deemed to have been normal.

What gives an insight into how he was mentally at that time, I refer to part of the first-ever conversation I had with him which took place via telephone only a few months ago. During that conversation, having learned of his silence for over 40 years, I said to him, "Gary, are you nuts? If someone had shot my eye out and blown half my face away, I'd have been screaming from the rooftops!" He said, "Tom, you didn't go through it. I was at the most vulnerable point in my life. I had a family and a young kid to support, knew I was severely disabled, and they said they'd keep me on. I was in a fog and would have gone along with anything." So, we must bear in mind what he said when considering his witness statement.

I believe we can assume his account is in the main accurate, but I question certain aspects. One of which is his use of the word 'accident.' What made him choose to refer to it as being an 'accident' that early on? After all, he could not have known for sure it was an accident. So why use the reference as opposed to perhaps, 'incident?'

Therefore, I must conclude the likelihood that Gary had been possibly influenced by others in his usage of 'accident', by those who had maybe either jumped to the conclusion of it being an accident or it fitted their narrative. The one who had an opportunity was Detective Chief Inspector James who wrote the witness statement on Gary's behalf.

Gary clearly states the exercise had been declared as being over and still Zaffir Mispha did what he did. Gary has told me that the vehicle he was in was not being used in the exercise. He also said that students had been only recently warned of the dangers of placing a gun close to a vehicle window and discharging it.

The most questionable part of Gary's statement is this in the closing part:

'In my opinion, the accident was probably caused by a .32 blank being inserted into a chamber followed by a .38 blank in the same chamber which has caused the .32 to be discharged like a bullet without a head. This is based on the fact that it is within my knowledge that the remains of a .32 blank case have been found in the damaged vehicle.'

There is no factual evidence in any form to support that opinion. Furthermore, the last sentence of that quote would have been inadmissible in any court proceeding because it is 'hearsay evidence' based on something he MUST have been told by someone. Once again, Detective Chief Inspector James had an opportunity. Who else could it have been?

Finally, we move to the report of Mr Greenwood, the firearms' expert. You must be made aware that he was commissioned by Gary's solicitor and not GMP to provide the report and that was nearly 18 months after the incident occurred.

Undoubtedly, he is well qualified to give his opinion. However, he is understandably unable to conclude as to why the incident took place. The gun and vehicle were never examined and even if they had been subsequently, I suggest all relevant forensics would likely have long since disappeared because there is no evidence of preservation.

On the facts available it seems that the 'thorough investigation' as quoted in the Manchester Evening News article was dubious to say the least, due to there being no evidence of forensic preservation of either the scene, van or gun.

Mr Greenwood does not agree with the theory of a .32 blank being involved but it appears the obvious need for testing of this and the impact of a blank being fired on or close to the vehicle window was disappointingly never carried out.

Therefore, without forensics or testing much will remain unknown and the only conclusions that can be made are on that which is known and not in dispute, which unfortunately is very little.

What seems indisputable is that the training lacked the care and discipline that should have been demanded. The students were on the whole mainly reckless and incompetent and should have been removed from the course at the first sign of dangerous behaviour.

Sadly, that was not done, and I submit that was because of the lucrative contract and the adverse effect it may have had on overseas relationships. It does seem to be the case that the course and in particular those students were a danger to be around and indeed an accident waiting to happen.

In my view, Gary cannot be blamed for any such breach of safety rules. He was neither in overall charge nor a fully qualified instructor, merely an authorised firearms user and a seconded aide. Furthermore, I would suggest that if he had been thought to be overly critical of the behaviour of the students or in any way demeaning the instructors and their lack of proper supervision and/or discipline, it would have been Gary who would have swiftly departed from the course and no one else.

I suggest that maybe he should not have even been present nor offered such an appointment by GMP in the first instance, given his lack of instructor qualifications but I hasten to add that did not contribute in any way to his being shot.

My conclusions are at this time that it appears likely that we will never know for certain how or why this tragic incident occurred. It may have been either a deliberate act to injure or a reckless and stupid act that went wrong.

What is odd is that if it was an accident then one would have expected Mispha to visit Gary in hospital or to have given, by some means, an apology of sorts but that was never offered or passed on via Detective Chief Inspector James or any member of the GMP.

Was GMP negligent in their responsibility to ensure safety rules were adhered to? Was GMP negligent in failing to implement a lockdown of the possible crime scene and preserve evidence? On the currently available evidence, it appears they were guilty on both counts.

Was there a total cover-up by the government and GMP? I do not think based on that known we can positively say so. What we do know from Gary is that he was ordered by a senior officer to remain silent.

However, in the reporter Steve Panter's article of 29 Jan. 1991, 8 years after the shooting, it states:

'As Gary recovered, he was visited by an assistant chief constable (ACC) who told him not to talk about the affair.'

Gary has no recollection of an ACC ever visiting him and even though on occasions he was sedated, both he and I think he'd recall that rare high-ranking visitor, if it ever happened. The only one who did visit him was Detective Chief Inspector James and maybe Steve Panter could have got his 'Chiefs' slightly confused. However, what I do believe is that Gary's silence was ordered and that likely could have only come from the one who visited him.

We must also not forget that the hospital staff confirmed they had been ordered by police into strict lockdown on revealing any information to anyone, including shockingly Gary's own wife. Gary himself was the first one to get a message sent out to her.

IMPORTANT REVELATION. 13 October 2024.

Today, on re-reading through the above, I thought of something, and I put this to Gary via a written message:

'At the time you were shot what was Detective Chief Inspector Dave James' role in GMP?

Did he have any part whatsoever in firearms/firearms instructing/the course in any way whatsoever?

Also, why him who visited you in the hospital AND took the statement from you later?'

This was Gary's response:

'Dave James was the Detective Chief Inspector in charge of the Firearms Department.'

This of course is significant to say the least, but I will let you, the reader, judge how much so.

Whilst it is not necessarily a requirement, good practice would dictate even at the time that this occurred that the matter should have been investigated independently. A suggestion would be that this involved the then equivalent of the Force's Professional Standards Department possibly overseen following a referral by the force to the Police Complaints Board which is what existed at the time (now the IOPC - Independent Office of Police Conduct). This did not happen. The implication will be obvious to the reader. Why was this allowed to take place?

My opinion is that somebody at a senior level and certainly higher than Detective Chief Inspector James, should have decided to organise for an independent investigation to take place. This could have involved another police force but at the very least independent officers from inside of the GMP.

Anyone can see that this matter should have been treated as being of the utmost importance. Two police officers were injured, one very seriously. Issues had been raised that what had taken place on the training course was not as professional as it should have been. The statement of the firearms' expert tells us that much. Therefore, there were implications for the force's reputation as well as the wellbeing of the officers involved and at the very least, lessons to be learned for the future.

Whether there was anything sinister regarding the outcome of the investigation such as it was, must unfortunately remain as speculation because there is insufficient evidence available to support such a suggestion. However, it does by inference leave the GMP and individuals within it susceptible to criticism at the very least.

I now have further questions in regard to the taking of Gary's witness statement by Detective Chief Inspector James. It is obvious that he was not by any stretch of the imagination independent and therefore it may have been prudent to have chosen another writer, one not connected to the firearms department.

Compare it if this were to happen:

If a factory worker were to be injured whilst working on a lathe, would it be acceptable for the manager/boss of the company to be the one who obtained the witness statement from the injured party and carried out the investigation into the accident, as opposed to an independent Health & Safety official?

Well of course it would be highly unacceptable and indeed unethical because the manager could be held responsible for any negligence, would not be independent and impartial and thus could influence the wording of the statement to his advantage. In addition, undoubtedly in this situation the manager/boss has his employee at a vulnerable and possibly submissive disadvantage.

It would strike you as being inappropriate for Detective Chief Inspector James himself to investigate the incident. It should either have been investigated by the then equivalent of the Professional Standards or referred to the then Police Complaints Board (PCB) for them to oversee the investigation which was available and should have happened in those times. However, we have no evidence available to support that was a course taken.

You recall I inferred the possible provision and influencing of the word 'accident' in Gary's witness statement and the sharing of the information of the possible connection with a .32 calibre blank cartridge case. Well, to me it all makes a lot more sense now!

However, what do you think?

Gary was never told of the outcome of any investigation either verbally or in any report or letter. To this day he does not know what, if any action, was taken against Mispha. He thinks he was allowed to carry on with the course and subsequently returned to Saudi.

When Gary returned to work nothing was ever mentioned. He

submissively and compliantly did not rigorously pursue the matter. He has said that he did not do so because he felt it best for his mental health and family that it was left alone. So instead, he chose to move on making the best of a bad job and focusing on the future.

With my guidance, Gary has made a 'Subject Access Request' (SAR) under the Freedom of Information Act 2000, to GMP. ALL information held on Gary, especially relating to his shooting has been requested.

To obtain any previously obtained statement of Mr Milner and Mispha may clarify much but any likelihood of that happening is in the hands of GMP. As previously mentioned, I am aware that Mr Henry Milner QPM sadly died a number of years ago.

Given the passage of time, 40 years, it remains to be seen what will be produced by GMP but if nothing further relevant is revealed then sadly it seems that the mystery and conspiracy theories will continue.

UPDATE. Today, 6 November 2024, GMP have replied to Gary's 'Subject Access Request' and the response is as anticipated.

Here is the quote from their letter:

Question. 'I am looking for any and all records of me being shot on 15th November 1983, any statements or interviews. I suppose anything in my record that relates to the incident and enquiry afterwards.'

Reply. 'GMP Systems and the relevant units have undertaken extensive searches for the data you have requested, and I can advise that we are unable to locate this data please note that this could be due to the time-lapse and GMP's weeding policy.'

Information Compliance & Records Management Unit.

NOTE. Kevin Moore and I had a prior agreement to independently view the limited evidence and to document our findings without divulging what they were, until after both were completed so as not to influence one another. You will read that our conclusions are similar.

BUT... what do you conclude?

CHAPTER 11

BREAKING NEWS.

Here is a fantastic full article printed in the Manchester Evening News.

NEWS ARTICLE 6 OCT 2024

Hero cop shot in eye and the astonishing cover-up that followed.

Officer's ordeal investigated in new book as his case helps spearhead campaign for injured emergency service workers.

By Neal Keeling.

Gary Pearson was a brave cop. Before a hushed-up shooting changed the course of his career he had shown his mettle at the sharp end of the thin blue line.

Ten days before he lost his left eye when it was shot out by a Saudi royal bodyguard during a training exercise Gary had been part of a team that arrested two men armed with a sawn-off shotgun who were about to commit a robbery on a family home.

On another occasion, he single-handedly arrested a gunman who was about to rob a pub in Swinton.

When fire engulfed the Woolworths' store in Manchester city centre on May 8th, 1979, he drove a car at a door to try and help trapped customers escape. Their screams haunted him.

But on November 15th, 1983, his life changed forever deep in the Kielder Forest in Northumberland close to the border with Scotland. What happened was kept a secret for seven years until he took GMP to court and received an out-of-court settlement and the Manchester Evening News then revealed the cover-up.

Now his ordeal will be the subject of a new book, and his case is helping to spearhead a campaign by an ex-policeman for the thousands of emergency workers from all three services who were forced to retire through injury to get the recognition they deserve.

At the time Gary, then aged 30, and living in Prestwich, was a Detective Constable, and an aid in the firearms' department. "We were in Kielder Forest near the Kielder Dam. We were training Saudi and Bahrain officers in anti-ambush techniques and firearms scenarios. They were police officers and the army.

The system in those countries is that they are more like paramilitary than police. We had gone up in a couple of personnel carriers. The exercise had finished, and I was sat in the front passenger seat of one.

This Saudi officer came running out from the bushes, opposite the van, fired a couple of shots which were blanks. He was eight to ten feet away when he first came out. Then he ran round to the driver's side and put the .38 revolver up to the window of the driver's side. Then there was this loud bang. The windows went in, and I felt as though someone had punched me in the face.

I put my hand up to the left-hand side of my face and put my finger inside my cheek and I realised I was quite badly injured. I believe he had inserted a .32 blank into the cylinder of the gun and then put a .38 after it. The .32 was the piece that came out like a bullet head. All of the cheekbone had gone.

The blank had gone into the eye socket and blown up the back of the eye which destroyed the optic nerve. There was a lot of tissue loss and bone loss. Doctors said they had to take out what was left of the eye as leaving it in would be a risk as it could affect the other eye, and I would go blind in the immediate aftermath of the incident." Gary and the hospital staff were told not to talk about it.

I was taken to hospital in Carlisle and my face was so badly swollen I couldn't see.

A nurse came in and said the hospital was in lockdown. They had been told not to tell anyone what had gone on and not to contact my next of kin, my wife.

"The nurse didn't think it was fair. I gave her my phone number and she rang my wife. After she had spoken to her my wife got a phone call from a senior GMP officer that had come up to Carlisle after they found out there had been a shooting. He said, "Your husband has got something in his eye." She wanted to travel up and he said, "Now, now, dear, let's not panic. I will let you know what happens."

After Gary had surgery and the extent of the injury, he had suffered was clear his wife was called by police and told to get to the hospital. She was not given a blue light lift in a police car but had to drive herself from Manchester to Carlisle with her two-year-old son. His wife and son walked past his hospital bed as his injuries were so bad they did not recognise him.

Gary said: "The welfare officer from the police up there arranged for her to stay at a nearby boarding house. She stayed there with my lad for close to a week before we were brought back down to Manchester. A couple of weeks after that I got a bill through the post from the GMP welfare department asking for over £200 for her stay. I paid it."

He added: "We had just bought our first home; the mortgage was very high, and I was dependent on my wage plus overtime. Now I was on the sick we were finding it pretty hard to manage financially.

"I contacted the head of welfare and told him I was paying into the force's insurance scheme and that it said for the loss of an eye you would get £5000, and it said there would be an immediate payout.

He stated it wasn't immediate payment and that I should either get a loan from a relative or ask my bank for a loan. I told him the advert on the poster near the armoury at Rochdale nick said 'immediate payouts' and I'd get the details from the notice. Colleagues and I searched every police station and not one advertisement poster could be found. They had all disappeared.

"Throughout all my stay in the hospital and my two months at home, I was never visited by police or welfare, not even a phone call."

He paid for his face to be rebuilt using titanium plates to replace the lost cheekbone, and his eye socket was repaired using flesh from inside his mouth.

"I eventually went back to work but only behind a desk. I spent the next 12-18 months in a fog. I put up with that and being in the office for the next 6 years. It was during this time that a detective inspector first referred to me as 'Cyclops'. I could have either punched him in the face and lost everything or leave the job I loved, I left.

"From being shot to leaving not one senior officer asked how I was or gave me any explanation as to why I had been injured. I was left to get on with it and keep my mouth shut. For someone to speak to me like that was out of order. It wasn't as if I was desk-bound all my career - I had been out and done it. I was part of the fabric of the firearms' department. I had been out risking life and limb, and you've got some limp-wristed individual calling you this. I joined the old Manchester and Salford force from school, which became GMP in 1974. I had always wanted to be a bobby," he said.

Asked whether he considered the shooting an accident or reckless behaviour he said: "I have always said I didn't want to think about anything which may start feelings of anger. I had a wife and a son and then my little girl came along. I didn't want to be in that position where I became bitter. So, I just thought, 'It's happened'. I did not realise until I spoke to Tom just how many bobbies are in the same position. My injury, I don't think, compared to some is that bad. He put it into perspective when he said to me, "A special constable can work for nine years and get a medal." So, if I am standing next to them at a Remembrance Day parade, he has a medal showing his years of service and I've got nothing. I did not get the years in for a long service medal.

"Even though I got the settlement, it is hard to explain the pain I am in all the time. When it gets cold it is worse. Because I have titanium plates where my cheekbone is - and the surgeon did a great job - your face becomes as cold as the weather outside. The pain is like if you crunch an ice cube and the numb pain afterwards. But it is continuous until I can warm my face up again. You just have to put up with it."

Tom has cross-party support for his campaign in Parliament with veteran MP Sir Roger Gale championing it plus the support of the Police Federation of England and Wales, the National Association of Police Officers, the Northern Ireland Police Federation and the main unions in the fire and ambulance service.

A spokesperson from Greater Manchester Police said: "As time has passed, substantial changes have been made to policing around provision and welfare of officers and staff. While it is of immense regret that Mr Pearson and his family were treated this way, we know that if an officer was to encounter an incident of this nature today, they would receive the very best care and support from the force.

"At the time of the incident, a thorough investigation was conducted, and a decision was made not to authorise charges against the involved parties."

Details of Tom's campaign can be found at:

facebook.com/groups/1415295802502023

AUTHOR'S COMMENT

This is a very well written and comprehensive article completed by a top professional reporter, Neal Keeling.

In 1991 Manchester Evening News were not afraid to be the first and only to break this story, when their reporter, Steve Panter, took it to print. Their assistance is very much appreciated.

It is worth noting that from the recent GMP spokesperson's comment above, that this is the first time Gary has come even close to receiving an apology from GMP. I believe that in itself is somewhat of an achievement.

However, I dispute the latter part of the statement that anything has changed as to improved care and welfare, based on the vast number of cases I can present.

CHAPTER 12

BOOK CONCLUSION

It has been a privilege and a unique, experience whilst collaborating with Gary to bring about this book.

Due to being at opposite ends of the country all our contacts throughout have been via email messaging or telephone, often making for arduous documentation and progress.

Gary remains an upbeat, magnanimous, personable man and a joy to speak with. I sincerely hope we will eventually meet in person soon.

Of the many horrific stories of the disgraceful overlooking and shocking treatment of emergency service personnel that have come my way, his is the worst of the worst and what inspired me to document and broadcast it. His catastrophic injuries and totally uncaring treatment make him a prime candidate for my medal proposal.

This brave former dedicated and professional police officer deserves the long overdue recognition for his police service, health and job sacrifice, along with many others.

However, I want all who read this to be aware that there are many 1000s more heartbreaking stories out there, across all emergency services, Gary's has just been one of them.

We are living through disturbing and turbulent times. Have no illusions about it, law and order are under attack with the police absorbing the brunt. More and more officers are being assaulted and injured every day.

From 30 July to 5 August 2024, far-right, anti-immigration protests and riots occurred in England and Northern Ireland, within the United Kingdom. This followed a mass stabbing in Southport on 29 July in which three children were killed.

During the riots, over 130 police officers were injured but what the nation needs to be made fully aware of is that if any of those unfortunate officers are subsequently medically discharged from the service, they too will receive no medal recognition whatsoever. Many who may not have reached the service eligibility period to qualify for the 'Long Service & Good Conduct Medal' i.e. 20 years, will leave with nothing to show even a connection to the service let alone their health and job sacrifice.

Until such times as there are permanent deterrents in place to safeguard our emergency service personnel against attacks they will continue to increase, as they are, at an alarming rate.

As long ago as the eighties, when Willie Whitelaw was the Home Secretary, he threatened to get tough on criminals when he introduced 'short, sharp, shock' youth detention centres. That did not work.

Prime Minister Keir Starmer during the riots called for harsher sentencing to quell the disturbances. It was swiftly implemented but at the cost of releasing 100s of prison inmates early under the serve only 40% of the sentence for good behaviour scheme. This was done to free spaces in the overcrowded prisons, making room for those newly sentenced for riotous behaviour.

It seemed to have had the desired effect, and the rioting stopped but some of those inmates released to make way were soon recalled to prison within days for breaking the rules of their parole licence.

I know from my time as a police goaler in the early eighties, when prison inmates were temporarily housed in police cells due to overcrowding, that just because an inmate's behaviour is good while behind bars it does not necessarily mean it will continue when released.

What is the point of imposing an imprisonment sentence for example of 5 years, if it's almost a foregone conclusion that the release will be after 2 years? As I stated, it's not a problem for many inmates to be of good behaviour whilst confined within a prison, it's maintaining it once returned to society when temptations are again presented.

What is needed and has been since the eighties is more new prisons and stiffer sentencing or we face even further escalation of crime and disorder. The more tolerant society becomes the more confident and frequent the offenders will become because they will have nothing to fear.

Therefore, all our emergency service personnel more than ever, need our full support in exchange for their dedicated service. They deserve our admiration and appreciation of any sacrifice made as a result of dangers they face on a daily basis to keep us, the public, safe. The least we can do is to honour the severely injured with a medal. It of course will not alter what happened or change any lives, but it will show the nation cares in a way that will have little or no effect on the all-important present-day budgets.

On 9 March 2024, the long overdue posthumous 'Elizabeth Emblem' was finally approved honouring the 'fallen' but again the injured were overlooked. How can you recognise the dead but not the injured, who may have come within a fraction of an inch of paying the ultimate sacrifice and frequently only because of the intervention of brilliant medical professionals? It simply does not make sense and is a national scandal that needs correcting without delay.

After the riots, the police were praised for their actions by the King and the government. However, we have long heard such propaganda claptrap circulated by those in power. Now we must demand action in bringing about proper medal recognition instead of more mere meaningless words.

I recently read the widely acclaimed book 'No Ordinary Day' co-written by Matt Johnson and John Murray. It tells of the murder of WPC Yvonne Fletcher outside the Libyan Embassy in London on 17 April 1984 and what took place in the aftermath.

John Murray who cradled Yvonne as she died that tragic day, is a member of my Facebook campaign group and we have spoken on a few occasions. I told John, "There is one sentence in your book I shall carry with me forever." It says, 'A barrel of oil is worth more than a police officer's life'.

I now realise that there appears to be more than just that 'barrel of oil' which is of greater importance to some. The statement could apply to any lucrative overseas' contract and especially police pension budgets.

On the evidence available, the same thinking appears to equally apply to severely injured police officers with life-changing injuries who narrowly escape paying the ultimate sacrifice.

Many of these officers have to fight the powerful system to gain their rightful injury pension awards but sadly far too often they are not successful and thus lose out financially for the remainder of their lives.

The system wants rid sure enough, of any officer once they have been injured and are of no further use. That I understand but without pity and involving skulduggery to achieve the aim as cheaply as possible, I have difficulty with that! By the way I have much evidence to support my claim.

I submit that the current merciless injury pensions administration is an even bigger ignominy than that of the lack of a medal. I believe one day the facts of the ruthless, lacking in compassion and flawed pensions system, which is focused entirely on budget saving and not on what is right and just, will be revealed. Then it will be viewed as being as scandalous as the recent Royal Mail fiasco.

However, the pensions disgrace is an entirely separate matter but the attitude to both pensions and the medal overlooking are a clear indication of how little regard there is for the fair treatment of the injured.

I believe that as of now, 26 November 2024, the campaign is right on track to succeed. It has support from the big 3 emergency service unions, along with many lesser. It has gained huge declared cross-party MP support, 80 currently and growing.

Matt Vickers the Shadow Crime, Police and Fire Minister has joined forces with Sir Roger Gale MP, and he too now champions the campaign.

During the week beginning 21 October 2024, Matt, from the floor of the House of Commons put a question to Yvette Cooper, the Home Secretary, asking to meet her with Tom Curry. The Home Secretary's response indicated support for the cause and was positive, a meeting may be imminent.

However, what I continue to find bizarre is that the chief constable of Sussex Police, Jo Shiner, and the National Police Chiefs' Council, after numerous approaches, still refuse to declare their support for the campaign, even though I have updated them as to the huge mounting support from others.

Perhaps, that dismissive and disinterested attitude coming from those you would not have expected, is a clear indication as to why nothing has ever been done in the past to correct this scandal.

The campaign fight will continue until it does succeed in correcting the 200-year-old national disgrace of the overlooking of the forgotten injured:

> *"And maybe remind the few,*
>
> *if ill of us they speak,*
>
> *that we are all that stands*
>
> *between the monsters and the weak".*
>
> *Michael Marks*

Finally, from me to my friend, Gary Pearson, 'Well done, lad. I salute you!'

Stay safe.

Tom Curry

THE FINAL WORDS ARE LEFT TO GARY

Gary Pearson

After viewing an email from the 'National Association of Retired Police Officers' telling of the national campaign to seek medal recognition for medically discharged police officers being led by former officer Tom Curry, I contacted him.

I had no idea what an incredible release of feelings this would have for me and my wife. Far from me thinking I was the only copper to be injured I now found there are hundreds of us.

After reading some of their sad stories, I realised that they all had the same theme, not one injured copper ever spoke of how the 'police family' had looked after them. This gave me pause to think about my own experience.

After my injury, I was not once contacted by police welfare other than a letter asking for a refund of the money they paid for my wife's stay at the boarding house in Carlisle. I never received any visits from senior police officers or even a phone call. It was never suggested I receive any form of help in case I had any mental issues and as my wife says, she had 5 years of hell not knowing what mood I would be in when she came home.

I must be honest and say that after reliving the incident for the purposes of this book I have been re-visited with the nightmares. My wife says I have again started to shout out in my sleep as I relive the incident in my dreams.

I sincerely believe in the efforts of Tom to get injured coppers the recognition that their injuries and sacrifices deserve and not the attitude of some in the police that they should be swept under the carpet and forgotten. Tom's broadcasting will go a long way to bring to notice the plight of injured coppers who have lost their own voices.

My main reason for giving my consent and sharing my story has been to promote Tom's brilliant campaign and to broadcast the suffering and overlooking of what the injured endure.

After a 'freedom of information request' to Greater Manchester Police asking for any information on me being shot, I received the reply that they had no record of the incident, no statements, no reports, no forensic report, nothing, I suppose that says it all.

I would like to express my sincere appreciation to Tom Curry for writing my biography and his tireless campaign efforts. I also thank Kevin Moore for his invaluable input and to all who contributed and helped to make this book possible.

If not for the support from my loving family my story may have been very different as I too felt totally let down by the police in their efforts to distance themselves from the incident.

My undying love and gratitude go to my caring wife and family who are always there for me. It is over 40 years since my shooting, and I have lived longer with the injury than without and thus it consumes little of my present-day thoughts.

Throughout the years, I truly believed no one outside of my family cared. I was wrong.

Gary Pearson

Books by the same author:

WOR TOMIS THE POLIS (Our Thomas the Policeman)

DYSFUNCTIONAL POLICE FAMILY ADD INSULT TO INJURY

Printed in Great Britain
by Amazon